KID BLACKIE

Jack Dempsey's Colorado Days

by Toby Smith

GW00673139

wayfinder
PRESS

Published by Wayfinder Press, P.O. Box 1877, Ouray, Colorado 81427

Editor: Jack Swanson
Cover Design: Clarke Cohu
Copy Editing: Janet Oslund
Typography: The Silverton Standard and The Miner
Lithography: Walsworth Press, Inc.

Illustration Credits:
   Richard Pipes - 15, 18, 21, 41, 80, 107, 119, 126, 135, 140.
   Denver Public Library, Western History Department - cover (center
   and upper left), 56, 93, 102.
   UPI - cover (right), 72.
   Rod Barker - 33.
   Marvin Gregory - 49.
   Eddie Bohn - 154.
   Mark Holm - back cover.
   Toby Smith - 151.
   Pueblo Library District - 135.

ISBN: 0-9608764-7-2

For a couple of Champs named Jed and Kit

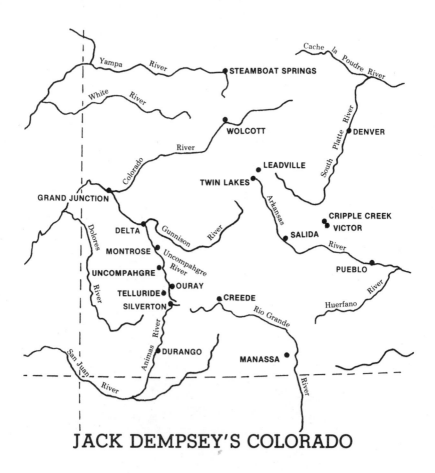

JACK DEMPSEY'S COLORADO

TABLE OF CONTENTS

INTRODUCTION

I never saw Jack Dempsey fight. I was born nineteen years after Dempsey's last heavyweight championship bout, the 1927 one in which he knocked down Gene Tunney in the seventh round and still lost. That was the famous "long count" decision.

My father used to tell me about the long count when I was a boy. He had listened to the fight, held at Chicago's Soldier Field, on the radio, as so many Americans had. The emotion surrounding that event, which he'd heard on a crackling Crosley from a small West Texas town, stayed with my father for years. The drama for some people was permanent: ten men across the country died from heart failure while listening to the long count.

Though I never saw Dempsey box, I knew about him. Like Babe Ruth, Red Grange, Bill Tilden and other sports greats of the 1920s, Dempsey was still talked about with awe long after he retired. As a schoolboy, I got into a playground scrap one day and was sent inside. "Who do you think you are?" the principal asked me sternly. "Jack Dempsey?"

Because I grew up about forty miles from New York City, Broadway's bright lights, which Dempsey first encountered in 1916 after leaving Colorado, attracted me on occasion. My teenage friends and I used to sneak through Times Square when our parents weren't looking. We often passed Jack Dempsey's restaurant.

Later, when I served in the Army, I entered the restaurant. I can still recall the address: 1619 Broadway. Inside, on one wall, hung the monumental James Montgomery Flagg painting of Dempsey chopping down towering Jess Willard to win the heavyweight title in 1919. The painting now graces the Smithsonian Institution.

Dempsey guarded the front window the day I went in. "How're ya doin', pal?" he'd greet strangers, shoving forth a hand the size of a catcher's mitt. In a few minutes, Dempsey came over to where my Army buddy and I sat. Puffy and jowly, but with hair still thick and dark, Dempsey leaned across our booth. "Where you fellas stationed?" he asked, his voice husky yet friendly.

We told him.

"What're your names?" he probed.

I gave mine. Then my Army friend, Eugene Daly, the Third Infantry Brigade's resident wit, said with a smirk, "It's Gene, Mr. Dempsey. *Gene.* That's a name you've probably heard before."

For a second I thought my heart might explode through my uniform shirtfront. *Of all the things to say, Daly! Why'd you have to bring up Gene Tunney?*

But Dempsey, even in his early seventies, knew how to take a punch—and how to return one. Rubbing his massive jaw, Dempsey stared a moment at Gene Daly.

"Was that Gene with a 'G' or a 'J'?" he boomed before moving on to another table.

Dempsey's popularity seems to grow as the years pass. In a 1986 address to the nation, President Ronald Reagan said, "Well, to those who think strength provokes conflict, Will Rogers had his own answer. He said of the world heavyweight champion of his day: 'I've never seen anyone insult Jack Dempsey.'"

Sometime during my youth, and I'm not exactly sure when, I heard Jack Dempsey referred to as "The Manassa Mauler." For years I assumed Dempsey had grown up in Manassas, Virginia, a fair-sized community southwest of Washington, D.C. Only after I moved to northern New Mexico in 1976 did I discover the whereabouts of Manassa: northeast of Chama, New Mexico, just across the state line in Colorado.

Information on Dempsey's early years, the days before he became a Great American Hero, is not abundant. Dempsey never talked much about the period; some of it was too painful. Though Dempsey is buried in New York City and probably most identified with that part of the country, Dempsey's early life—the days he didn't talk much about—took place in Colorado.

Those were important years for him, maybe the most important of his life. During that time he grew as a boxer and as a man. Living on his own from age fifteen, Dempsey learned to fight in towns across southern and central Colorado, towns that were so wild and woolly Bibles were sold under the counter. He also learned to dig for gold, hop freights, pick fruit, wash dishes and mop floors. From 1911 to 1916 Dempsey barnstormed from one Colorado mining camp to another, from one railroad crossing to the next. Often he traveled as an itinerant fighter who called himself "Kid Blackie." Nobody knows for sure how many fights Kid Blackie had. Scores took place in gin mills and never were recorded by the press or sanctioned by the law.

Years of slugging it out for meal money in rough-and-tumble Colorado communities, months of sleeping under bridges and sweeping out hallways, hardened in Dempsey's mind his life's ambition: to win the heavyweight title. When he did win it in 1919, the American public gasped, for it had never seen such a savage brawler. Indeed, Dempsey did not just beat Jess Willard on July 4, 1919, he destroyed him. The young man from Colorado snapped Willard's jaw, pried loose six teeth, broke his cheekbone, squashed his nose, closed one eye swollen shut, and painted the champion in blood.

The early years of Jack Dempsey/Kid Blackie then are significant not just in terms of boxing, but in terms of living—and learning to never give up on a dream. In moving from poverty to Park Avenue, Dempsey became the first and perhaps truest fistic Horatio Alger, the kind of hero that historian Frederick Jackson Turner said resulted directly from the Western frontier.

Dempsey's health began to fail in 1978, not long after his old foe Gene Tunney died. Dempsey was eighty-seven when he died of natural causes in his Manhattan apartment. The date was May 31, 1983. He left a reputation for having the most profound killer instinct of anyone in boxing history.

But Dempsey is remembered too with great affection. He was a champion who could be enormously human, even in defeat. When he fought Gene Tunney in the controversial long count, before an audience of 102,000, and kept Tunney on the canvas for a reported fourteen seconds and didn't win, Dempsey shrugged at the outcome. "It was just one of the breaks," he said afterward. "Tunney fought a smart fight."

Sportsmanship, courage, pride, patriotism, resourcefulness and determination all were characteristics that

Dempsey acquired in Colorado's Rockies. In Colorado, Dempsey found great disappointment as well as great desire. What he learned from both would serve him well later. He never forgot his roots.

To understand Jack Dempsey, one must understand his early days in Colorado, from his birth in the state in 1895, until his twenty-first year there—the period covered in this book. I have traced those two decades through interviews with people who remember Kid Blackie and through the fragments of material that, as tiny scars on a prizefighter's face, have sat silently for years waiting to be studied.

My research and examination of those scars reveal that Colorado not only provided Jack Dempsey with a beginning, but Colorado also gave him a destiny.

TOBY SMITH
Albuquerque

CHAPTER I

Manassa

"Sometimes he'd win and sometimes he'd take a whopping."

Traveling the single main street of Manassa, Colorado, a visitor sees a tidy row of whitewashed homes with manicured lawns, the Manassa Hardware, the Capital Theatre, the Jack Dempsey Birthplace and Museum, and the biggest building in town: the buff-colored brick Church of Jesus Christ of Latter-day Saints (the LDS church).

It is probably safe to say that if it were not for that church, which stands at the east end of Manassa, then the orderly houses, the hardware store, the theater and certainly the Jack Dempsey Birthplace would not exist.

Save for a small contingent of Hispanics who worship at St. Teresa's (the only other church in the village of one thousand), Manassa is a Mormon community. There are no taverns in town, only a single eatery, the Corner Cafe, which serves a respectable chicken-fried-steak dinner for $6.50.

Mormons first came to Colorado's San Luis Valley, a one-hundred-by-seventy-mile basin surrounded by majestic mountains, in 1878. That year a wagon train of seventy-two LDS members from Alabama and Georgia arrived to make new homes on the frontier. Most had come because of a missionary named John Morgan, who had toured the South and preached the virtues of the West. When the Mormon converts saw the arid new promised land that sat at an altitude of 7,600 feet, the pioneers named the place after Manasseh, the Old Testament son of Joseph of ancient Israel. Those Mormons who didn't settle in Manassa laid down roots in nearby Ephraim, Manasseh's biblical brother, or in Los Cerritos, another close-by community.

Historically, the first settlers in the area were not Mormons, but Spanish. Today, Manassa is rimmed by such towns as San Acacio, Alamosa, Del Norte, La Jara, La Garita and the previously mentioned Los Cerritos. Many Manassa residents grow up speaking two languages. (Long after Jack Dempsey left Manassa he could still understand some Spanish.)

Two years after the initial group of Mormons reached Manassa, Jack Dempsey's parents arrived. They had left Logan County, West Virginia, where they had been influenced by a Mormon missionary and converted to the LDS church. Hyrum Dempsey, a nomadic schoolteacher, his wife, Celia, and their two children guided a prairie schooner through dust storms, breakdowns and a lack of water in search of a better life in Colorado.

A dreamer and egotist, Hyrum Dempsey was of Scot-Irish ancestry. He had a high-pitched voice, which his most famous son inherited, and a lazy streak, which that son did not. Hyrum accepted the Mormon faith, at least at first. Later, he confessed, ''I know the church is right. I'm just too weak to live up to their rules.''

Tall and rail-thin, Hyrum was no athlete. However, *his* father, ''Big'' Dempsey, a formidable-looking county sheriff, had been a West Virginia regional boxing champion. Hyrum was no coward, though; he once went after a bear with an ax. But music was Hyrum's favorite activity. A fiddler, he played ''Turkey in the Straw'' the way some folks today watch television: all day long.

Tiny and wiry, Celia Dempsey was everything her husband was not: ambitious, loving, sacrificing, hard-working and religious. She embraced the Mormon tenets and drilled principles of honesty and good citizenship into her children. Of Cherokee and Choctaw lineage, Celia gave her son her high cheekbones and cinder-black hair.

Like the settlers before them, the Dempseys learned endurance in Manassa. Hyrum took whatever job he could find: laborer, mill attendant, farmhand. He'd hire on for a while, then quit. Meanwhile, Celia ran the house, which grew rapidly. By the time Jack was born—June 24, 1895—the Dempseys had eight other children. There would be eleven children in all. Two would die in infancy.

Jack Dempsey's birth certificate reads ''William Harrison Dempsey.'' He was named, as were many children of that time, after a president—in his case, William Henry Harrison. As a boy, Dempsey was called ''Harry,'' and sometimes ''Willy.'' When he reached his teens and began to box, he took the name ''Jack.''

Though Manassa has found a home for its favorite son, some travelers have trouble finding it.

Dempsey weighed 11 pounds at birth. As a boxer in his prime, he weighed 190 pounds and stood six-foot-one in height. However, Dempsey did not begin to grow until the last stage of his teenage years. When that happened, he surpassed in size his parents and all his siblings.

Manassa has always sat in a rugged agricultural belt. The growing season is short and the winters are long. Chief resources include alfalfa, field peas, hay, oats, spring wheat and livestock. After building an undistinguished little stucco house and surrounding it with a tattered picket fence, Hyrum Dempsey began to scratch out a living in the new land.

Though the Dempseys were poor—Jack never had a store-bought toy as a child; he used scraps of wood as substitutes—the family always had enough to eat, thanks to the Church Relief Society. Periodically, a Mormon "teacher," or lay preacher, visited the Dempseys to see how they were doing. If their cupboards appeared bare, a food basket would be sitting on the family's doorstep the next morning. The Mormons of Manassa, Jack Dempsey later explained, practiced the Good Neighbor Policy. "If people

15

around the corner needed help," Dempsey said, "you helped."

Dempsey was christened at age eight in the big, white San Luis Stake House, forerunner to the buff-colored church building. Dempsey went to Sunday school, and the family said grace before meals and held evening prayers. Celia Dempsey was responsible for much of this. At best, her husband was a "Jack Mormon" who drank whiskey and coffee, smoked, and indulged in other vices.

Jack Dempsey may have grown up penniless in Manassa, where he lived until he was ten, but he did not grow up unhappy. He learned to ride a horse almost before he learned to walk. He spent summers at Dead Man's Gulch, a swimming hole on the nearby Conejos River. During the fall he explored Devil's Kitchen, a rocky pinnacle on the bank of Little River, south of Manassa. In colder months he hung around the Haynie Store or Rogers' Blacksmith Shop.

However, even in stormy weather the Dempsey children were often outside. "*Pshaw*," Celia Dempsey used to tell neighbors. "The rain and wet won't hurt 'em. They need it just as much as the trees and flowers." And curiously, the Dempseys seldom had colds or were sick. "They're growing," said Celia, "as nature meant 'em."

No matter the season, Jack Dempsey occasionally got into fights. His brother Bernie, nearly twenty years older, taught Jack to box in Manassa by first teaching him to make a fist. The thumb, explained Bern, belonged outside the hand, not stuck inside.

Once a chum from Manassa's White House School, where Dempsey studied, gave Jack a wad of paper wrapped around a bullet and encouraged him to throw the paper into the school's stove. When the shell exploded, Dempsey received a willowing from his teacher. Dempsey responded by thrashing his playmate. Another time, when he was about seven, Dempsey got into a fight with a boy named Fred Daniels. A crowd that included Fred's father gathered to watch. "Bite him, Fred!" encouraged the senior Daniels. Fred paused to look at his father for a moment. When he did, Dempsey took the opportunity to land a crunching blow on his opponent's chin. Said one spectator of young Fred: "He had to be revived by the local veterinarian."

Yet some old-timers in Manassa remembered Dempsey as a little boy who shunned fights. "Willy the Sissy," a few called him, for he loved birds (a hobby as an adult was hunting birds' nests) and was a bit of a mama's boy.

One Manassa boxing story, apocryphal perhaps, occurred several weeks before Dempsey was born. Arriving at the Dempsey home, a peddler begged Celia Dempsey to let him in the house to get warm. The peddler told Mrs. Dempsey that he had traveled a great distance and was exhausted and hungry. Mrs. Dempsey gave the man some milk, food and a blanket. Soon he took a nap. When he awoke, the peddler insisted on paying Mrs. Dempsey.

"I can't let you do that," she responded.

"Then look in my bag of wares," the peddler said, "and choose something for yourself."

Blindly, she selected a book entitled *Life of a 19th Century Gladiator*, an 1889 moralistic biography of the famous bareknuckle fighter John L. Sullivan.

The book allegedly enthralled and captivated Celia Dempsey. Throughout the remainder of her pregnancy she read such lines as these: "The lessons taught by the career of John L. Sullivan are lessons that every man will be better for learning. The experiences of this magnificent machine of flesh and blood are valuable in showing things that should certainly be avoided, as well as things that may profitably be copied."

When her son William Harrison Dempsey was brought into the world by a midwife who earned twenty-five cents, Celia Dempsey, legend has it, announced to him, "You will grow up to be the world's champion fighter. Just like John L. Sullivan."

Hyrum Dempsey died in 1948 in Salt Lake City, where the family had settled many years before. Dempsey did not attend his father's funeral. "I wanted to remember him as he had been, before all the arguments, the whiskey and the disillusionments. For too many years he had hurt my mother."

Celia Dempsey, whom Hyrum divorced several years after the Dempseys left Manassa, died in 1946. To the end she remained a strong woman, a John L. Sullivan fan who was unafraid to face the future. When she lay ill in a Salt Lake City hospital, Mrs. Dempsey was asked by a doctor, "Do you feel any better now?" Turning to the physician, Celia Dempsey snapped, "You know very well I'm dying. If you ask me how I feel again I'll get up out of this bed and punch you in the nose."

Luther Bagwell of Manassa: "Boxing was the only amusement we had as kids."

Of the many people who knew Jack Dempsey from his birth in Manassa until his family left the town in 1905, only one survives. Luther Bagwell, born in 1890, lives in a white-with-green-trim house just off Manassa's Main

Street. Bagwell's home is like most in Manassa: neat as frost on a fence post.

The barrel-chested Bagwell has the large, calloused hands and broad leathery face of someone who spent a life outdoors. A cattle rancher, Bagwell still feeds his cows each day. Taking time out from that chore, he pulls up a comfortable armchair in his living room and says that his parents came from Georgia to Manassa about the same time Dempsey's did: 1880. Hispanic natives of the area took care of the Bagwells and other Mormon colonists that first winter one hundred years ago. "Otherwise we'd have died."

Because he was six years older than Dempsey, Luther Bagwell was more friendly with Bern Dempsey than with Jack. "Jack tried to follow us everywhere," Bagwell says, tugging at the brim of a big, gray cowboy hat that seldom leaves his head. "If we went to the swimming hole, Jack would want to go and I'd have to chase him back." Occasionally, Bagwell consented to play a game of keeps or marbles with Dempsey.

According to Bagwell, every Manassa child ninety years ago learned to use his fists. "Boxing was about the only amusement we had as kids. If I didn't get in a fight every day at school, something was wrong. I saw Jack in lots of scrapes. Sometimes he'd win and sometimes he'd take a whopping."

Hyrum Dempsey left a poor impression on Bagwell. "He hated to work too hard. Simple as that. Later on, he dropped Jack's mother for a young woman in Utah." Jack Dempsey, however, left a much different mark on Bagwell. "What I liked most about Jack was how he took care of his mother after his father left her."

Though Dempsey offered free meals at his New York City restaurant to anyone from Manassa, Luther Bagwell never made it to Broadway. He did once ride a train from Philadelphia to Fairmont, West Virginia, and was mistaken for Dempsey during the journey. "I guess I looked a little like Jack."

Because he never owned a radio until recently, Bagwell followed Dempsey's fights mainly through the newspaper in Antonito, Colorado, twelve miles south of Manassa. (Oddly, when Dempsey beat Jess Willard for the title in 1919, the Antonito *Ledger* put the story on page five.) "I thought it was wonderful when Jack became champion," says Bagwell. "Lots of people here forgot all about him after the family moved on. But when Jack made it big, most were quick to claim him."

Dempsey returned to Manassa in July 1966 for a Pioneer Days celebration that would honor the opening of his boyhood home as a museum. More than five thousand people—one came from Denmark—turned out for the festivities, which included a parade. Dempsey stayed that weekend in Manassa with Harley and Janice Gilliland. Janice is Luther Bagwell's granddaughter. There are, in fact, about forty Bagwells in Manassa. Luther's son, LaVere, made a speech dedicating the museum. A curious thing happened at the Gillilands. By accident, Dempsey packed in his suitcase a towel belonging to his hosts and took it with him to New York. He later mailed it back, with a note of apology. Chuckling, Luther Bagwell says, "He was so embarrassed over that towel. His mother did a good job with him."

Jack Dempsey Day was the first time Dempsey had returned to Manassa in many years, and the last time he ever would. During the celebration, he asked about Mooney Daniels, playmate Fred Daniels' brother. "Mooney Daniels, growled Dempsey, "was the only boy in Manassa I was never able to lick."

———————

None of the Daniels boys are around today, but Jack Dempsey's birthplace, a one-room cabin, is still standing. Ever since it became a museum, the house has battled to survive in its off-the-beaten-path location. When Manassa turned Dempsey's birthplace into a tourist attraction, a big sign went up on U.S. 285, a moderately traveled highway three miles west of Manassa. The Colorado Highway Department has since ordered Manassa to remove the billboard. Therefore, if a motorist is not looking for Manassa, chances are he won't find it. But even if he does happen to pass through the town, he may not locate the house of its most famous son. The only road sign indicating its whereabouts is a small Point of Interest marker.

If Manassa sounds unwilling to promote the man who put the hamlet on the map, such is not the case. The village tries. When it resurrected Hyrum Dempsey's stucco shack, the town moved it to a pleasant, tree-shaded park and covered the house with logs to give it an Abe Lincoln look. The town painted the cottage cherry red and replaced the fireplace with windows. Not long ago, however, the twenty-by-thirty-foot house was in need of a makeover: the paint was peeling and the ersatz shingles were in disrepair.

"We just don't have any extra money," says Gay Williams, the Manassa city clerk and the museum's chief caretaker. "We take a loss on the home every year. Any money we get goes to the girls who work there."

The museum, which is open only from Memorial Day until school starts in late summer, is staffed by local teenage girls. There is no admission charge; donations are accepted. It's not certain, however, that the museum would profit even if visitors *were* charged. Last year donations totaled less than one hundred dollars. While sightseers average about four hundred per season, there are several days when no one visits.

In two glass display cases rest an old spinning wheel, an antique ear trumpet and an ancient typewriter, among various heirlooms. None of the objects came from the Dempsey family, as one might think, but from other

The Dempsey Museum in Manassa provides a wide range of boxing memorabilia and historical artifacts.

pioneers in the region. "Actually," says Gay Williams, "there's little here that belonged to the Dempseys. They didn't live in Manassa very long. And they were too poor to have much."

Another problem the museum faces is that not everyone in the area is enamored with Dempsey. Though most of Manassa recognizes the achievements of the boxer, some citizens point out that as he grew older, Dempsey drifted a bit from the Mormon religion. Photographs in the museum show Dempsey posing with different wives, smoking cigars, and holding a glass that probably did not contain Dr Pepper.

Dempsey, however, always maintained great fondness for Mormonism, even if he never adhered to the faith completely as an adult. "You know," he once told a friend, "I'd have become a Catholic but for one thing. The Mormons who helped my family so much would turn over in their graves."

The dearth of visitors and funds undoubtedly accounts for the lack of organization. Printed materials in the museum cover a broad range of topics. An article on Dempsey from the *Bangor* (*Maine*) *Daily News* shares space with a New Jersey Boxing Writers Award for 1965. Several photographs in the home bear no identification. And yellowed, Dempsey-related clippings decorate the walls in no particular sequence. A Cleveland (Ohio) *Plain Dealer* front page for July 5, 1919, with the banner headline "DEMPSEY KNOCKS OUT JESS WILLARD," hangs alongside a feature from London's *Sunday Express* that is headed "HE'S 67—BUT THEY STILL CALL HIM CHAMP."

The museum owns a pair of Dempsey's hightop black boxing shoes and the battered gloves he used in defending his heavyweight title against Luis Firpo in 1923, as well as several miscellaneous items: a stuffed bald eagle, a 1938 calendar, and a photograph of Lovie Gallegos, Colorado's Mother of the Year of 1982. There is no mention anywhere of Kid Blackie, the name Dempsey used when he started out as a fighter in Colorado.

The museum's teenage docents are cheerful and anxious to please, however. When asked how Dempsey acquired the nickname "The Manassa Mauler," Shelly Johnson made a telephone call and then reported that sportswriter Damon Runyon concocted the name. Ms. Johnson, who is Luther Bagwell's grandniece, can be forgiven for not readily knowing the answer; she goes to school at La Jara, Colorado.

Manassa's high school closed its doors in 1964. If Manassa High had still been in existence, Ms. Johnson would have known that its mascot was "The Mauler." Today, a big "M" sits on a mountain south of town.

"We know the Dempsey home could be better," says Gay Williams. "We certainly don't want to close it. We need it here. Jack Dempsey means so much to us."

And he thought a great deal of them.

CHAPTER II

Creede, Steamboat Springs, Delta

"I wish I'd kept that balloon."

"It was hard in Manassa," Dempsey recalled of the family's twenty-odd years along the Conejos River. "But I'm certain we were never again as secure as we were there."

About 1905, Hyrum Dempsey grew restless, the same feeling he'd earlier had in West Virginia. His dream of striking it rich, which he thought would happen in Colorado, was not being fulfilled in Manassa. Learning of a gold boom in Creede, Colorado, Hyrum sold everything the Dempseys owned, which wasn't much, and announced that the clan was moving on. Packing a wagon and some horses, the Dempseys headed eighty-five miles west to a spot not far from Wagon Wheel Gap on the Continental Divide. "One day we were in Manassa," said Jack, "and the next day we were gone."

When Hyrum didn't become a millionaire overnight in Creede, his wife pooled the family resources and opened a boardinghouse. She took in washing on the side.

Located at the headwaters of the Rio Grande, Creede was not the sort of place the devout Celia Dempsey preferred to raise her children. In those days, Creede was a colorful community with an even more flamboyant past. Bat Masterson had once served as town marshal. Calamity Jane dealt faro there. Creede was home of Soapy Smith's celebrated gaming tables and of Bob Ford, slayer of Jesse James. Eventually Ford was shot in a Creede saloon called The Candle.

Creede was more than colorful; it was often dangerous. Supposedly four out of every ten people living there at the turn of the century were fugitives from justice. Thirty saloons existed in a town with hardly any law and order. Founded in 1890, Creede became known across the country not only for its great mineral strikes, but for newspaper publisher Cy Warm's verse:

For it's day all day in the daytime.
And there is no night in Creede.

Creede was like many Colorado gold camps—from Central City to Crested Butte—that came into being in the 1880s and that Jack Dempsey came to know as a young man. Creede and the other camps of that era were not clean. Disease and unsanitary conditions abounded. And like most mining centers, Creede was remotely located. To reach it, the Denver and Rio Grande Railroad, which arrived in Creede in 1891, had to precariously chug up the side of a mountain.

The Dempseys settled on the outskirts of Creede in a place called Bachelor. Bachelor included a string of cabins above the mines. Because the cabins were scattered among the old stumps left by timber cutters, Bachelor also went by the name of "Stumptown."

Dempsey renewed his interest in boxing at Creede. Bern Dempsey, now a struggling amateur fighter, taught his brother how to stand and how to lead. Bern also introduced Jack to Andy Malloy, a prizefighter who came over Slumgullion Pass to Creede now and then. Malloy would later accompany Dempsey, billed as "Kid Blackie," across Colorado for boxing exhibitions.

A local character named Buck Belcher owned one of the few pairs of boxing gloves in Creede during that time. It was not unusual for Belcher to stand on a street corner and challenge passersby.

Boxing gloves might have been rare in Creede, but fistfights were not. One of the most famous involved two women. The women's husbands arranged the slugfest after the two ladies had engaged in name-calling for several weeks. When the women went at it, they clawed and scratched one another for hours on a public thoroughfare. Finally, one of the women sat down and mentioned to her opponent that she had some beer on ice at home.

"Let's go then," the other woman said. And so they exited, leaving their stunned husbands and a large crowd on the street.

Celia Dempsey's Creede boardinghouse did well. Some weeks Mrs. Dempsey took in as much as fifty dollars. Although expenses were high, she managed to save money, much more than her husband did. During the year the Dempseys spent in Creede, Jack realized how hard-working his mother really was. And how unlucky.

Dissatisfied over his lack of success in the mines, Hyrum Dempsey pulled the family out of Creede in 1906. There were other Colorado towns he wanted to see. Again Hyrum sold most of the Dempseys' belongings, save for a wagon, tent and some horses, gathered his wife and five of their youngest children (the older ones, including Bern, had left the nest by now) and headed north. Once more there was little planning and only a vague itinerary.

The trail out of Creede was not easy. Near Leadville, another robust mining camp, Jack Dempsey tried to cross the Arkansas River on horseback. His horse slipped on rocks and Jack fell into icy water. Although the water was not deep, the current was swift. Fortunately, Joe Dempsey reached in to pull out his younger brother. Jack was half-drowned, bruised and nearly frozen.

For a few months the Dempseys hung out in Leadville, almost two miles above sea level. A rugged frontier town, Leadville seemed to Celia Dempsey no less dangerous than Creede. Although the older Dempsey males got jobs at the Leadville rail yard for four dollars a day, the money did not outweigh the perils of this Wild West town. Typhoid and smallpox epidemics raged in Leadville. Pneumonia deaths were common from breathing the freezing thin air. Lawlessness was everywhere, as were mine accidents and work strikes. The housing was deplorable and a sewage system almost nonexistent.

When economic conditions began to plummet in Leadville, and the violence and difficulties of living in the town began to wear on the family, the Dempseys moved on.

South of Leadville a blizzard struck the Dempsey caravan. Snow and ice pelted their wagon and horses. Soon, Celia Dempsey grew ill. As each mile passed, the high altitude made her sicker. At Twin Lakes, Colorado, near the source of the Arkansas River, a worried and desperate Hyrum Dempsey decided to break up the family. Celia, Jack and two smaller children would return to Leadville and catch a train to Denver. There Celia would recuperate at the home of her married daughter, Florence. Pressing on, Hyrum and the others would meet up with them later.

At Leadville, Mrs. Dempsey bought one ticket, all she could afford, on the narrow-gauge Denver and Rio Grande Railroad. As the Dempseys settled into their train's thick yellow cushions, comforted by the warmth of a big iron stove

This James Montgomery Flagg painting hung in Dempsey's New York City restaurant for many years.

at the end of the car, a burly, red-faced conductor stopped at their seat.

Mrs. Dempsey gave the man her one ticket. Taking it, he glanced at the two youngest Dempseys, Elsie and Bruce. The conductor showed no expression. Then he studied Jack, now almost eleven. "I'll have to collect half-fare for him," the ticket-taker said.

"But I have no money," Mrs. Dempsey replied. "And I'm not well."

"You need to buy him a ticket," the conductor replied irritably, "or you're all off the train."

Celia Dempsey pleaded. She opened her empty purse and promised to repay the man someday. The conductor was unmoved. "Rules are rules," he barked with all the warmth of a chain gang boss. "Have the fare when I get back—or else."

A large gent in a ten-gallon hat sat across the aisle from the Dempseys. "I'll be glad to help you folks out," the cowboy offered. Then, winking at Jack, the stranger said, "But I'll bet you my horse that that conductor is bluffing."

The cowboy was right. When the conductor returned he did not stop at the Dempseys' seat or even look at the family.

Years later Dempsey listed the incident as one of the most

humiliating in a childhood filled with humiliating incidents. In Creede, everyone had struggled. On the train, the Dempseys were the only people wearing ragged clothing and shoes stuffed with paper. And they were the only ones without money. Dempsey vowed that what happened in Leadville would never be repeated when he grew up: he'd always be able to pay his way.

Mrs. Dempsey grew stronger after a few weeks in Denver. During her recovery, Hyrum sold the remaining good horse, wired seventy-five dollars to his wife, and instructed her to rejoin him in Wolcott, Colorado, about seventy miles north of Twin Lakes.

From Wolcott, the reunited Dempseys plodded north again, this time to Steamboat Springs, Colorado, where all the Dempsey males, Jack included, signed on as farmers' helpers. Ten-year-old Jack became a wheat baler. Then it was on to Mount Harris, a few miles west of Steamboat, for more farm work. Next the family migrated to Craig, Meeker and Rifle, Colorado.

During this 1906-1907 odyssey, Bern Dempsey had been in Utah working odd jobs and hunting up boxing matches. Deciding to hop a freight train back to Colorado to look for employment in the mines of that state, Bern got off the train in Rifle. He was walking down the main street of Rifle one afternoon when he came upon a crowd watching a scuffle between several young boys. One of the boys was Bern's little brother Jack. "That's how I discovered the family," Bern said. "Through a fight."

Pulling Jack aside, Bern asked him, "Harry, what're you doing?"

"I want to be a prizefighter," Jack answered, wiping dirt from his face. "Like you."

"I sure ain't earning many prizes fighting," Bern responded with a smile.

"Then I'll have to be better than you." Jack said, dusting his britches.

Bern put an arm around his brother's shoulder. "C'mon," he said. "Let's find the rest of the family."

The Dempseys stayed in northwest Colorado for about six months. The children went to school when they could. "It wasn't easy," remembered Jack. "The teacher was usually too busy keeping order to have much time for teaching." Mostly they worked: chopped wood, milked cows, cleared away manure, collected eggs from the farmer on whose land they stayed. No chores, commanded Celia Dempsey, no food.

Mrs. Dempsey was tough but loving. She was, Dempsey admitted, responsible for a lot of the fight in him. She preached the virtues of honesty every passing day. "If you can't look at yourself straight in the eye with respect in the morning after you've done something," she told her son, "then it means I've done a bad job and you aren't fit."

On occasion the family played. In Routt County, Colorado, eleven-year-old Jack and some of his siblings tried skiing. The novelty didn't last long. The barrel staves they used for skis became toboggans, which were more fun, especially when harnessed to the family's old jackass. In Meeker, that jackass came in quite handy when Jack needed a tooth pulled. Mrs. Dempsey knotted one end of a string inside her son's mouth and the other end to the ass's tail. Then she gave the animal a whack on the rump.

Winding their way south, the Dempseys, in mid-1907, came to Delta, Colorado, a county seat located at the fork of the Gunnison and Uncompahgre rivers. Delta stands at the gateway to the Grand Mesa, the largest flattop mountain in the world. Within its boundaries are more than two hundred lakes, many of which sit in ancient volcanic craters. The Grand Mesa now is a popular recreational playground. In the Dempseys' day it was simply hard country.

By the time the family reached Delta, Hyrum Dempsey's wanderlust had pretty well quieted. Offered a job in the Delta Brickyard, he decided to remain in the community. Jack even tried to earn a few extra nickels by hawking the *Saturday Evening Post* and the *Ladies Home Journal* on Delta's mud-choked streets.

Delta, however, was not receptive to the Dempseys. The town, in fact, had a history of orneriness. Only a few years before, some Deltans tried to hold a public lynching; they were stopped at the last moment. Many citizens in town felt that the dirt-poor Dempseys were undesirable and that Delta would end up taking care of the family. One evening, two prominent Delta residents came to the cabin the Dempseys were renting.

"We'd appreciate it if you'd move on," one of the Delta emissaries said.

The man's words stung Jack, who hovered near the door. The order hurt nearly as much as the incident on the Leadville train. Again Dempsey resolved that when he got older he'd have money—more money than his parents.

———————

Not everyone in Delta disliked the Dempseys. Jack gained one friend in Carl Smith, a thin blond youth who lived on a mesa overlooking town.

His hair the color of icicles and his shoulders sagging from his nine decades, Carl Smith now lives in the San Juan Living Center, a nursing home in Montrose, Colorado, twenty miles south of Delta.

Until a few years ago, Smith had spent all his life in Delta. He was, he says, the third boy born in the community. Smith's family had come to Delta from Illinois. His father raised and sold racehorses in western Colorado. When the Dempseys resided in Delta, only one country school existed in town and both Dempsey and Carl Smith attended it.

*His family's poverty never ceased to bother
Dempsey, particularly as a schoolboy in Delta.*

"Jack wasn't a troublesome or quarrelsome boy," Smith remembers. "He was real good-natured, considering how bad off his family was."

What Smith best recalls from that period was the time he brought to school a brand-new, bright blue balloon. The Cole Brothers Circus had recently passed through Delta, and Smith's parents had bought their son the toy there. The following day at school Dempsey started punching the balloon, perhaps out of frustration, Smith senses, at not being able to afford to go to the circus.

"Suddenly the balloon broke," Smith says, raising his frail arms out of his wheelchair in excitement. "Jack cried, 'I'll get you another one! I'll get a dime from Mama!'"

His eyes misting at the memory, Smith says that Dempsey didn't buy him another balloon. "That really doesn't matter now. I wish I'd kept that balloon. It was probably the first punching bag Jack Dempsey ever hit."

During World War I and after, Smith served in the Army as a band musician. He played the flute, tuba and clarinet. At one point Smith was stationed at Fort Lewis, Washington. One day Dempsey came to the base to put on a boxing exhibition.

"This was just before the time when some people were saying Jack was a slacker, a draft dodger," Smith says. "I don't know about any of that business. I do know that he put on a good show for us boys in uniform. The guy he fought might as well have stayed in bed."

CHAPTER III

Uncompahgre

"I mean, he was just a real country boy in them days."

From Delta the Dempseys moved south to a wide spot in the road eight miles below Montrose. The village, now gone, was known as Uncompahgre, a distortion of the Ute Indian word "Ancapogari," meaning "red lake." The Utes gave this name to the Uncompahgre River, which flows nearby, because its origin was a spring of reddish, bitter-tasting water.

Although Uncompahgre was located only 175 miles west of Manassa, it took the Dempseys almost two years to get there.

The high, dry Western Slope of the Continental Divide, where Uncompahgre lay and where the Dempseys spent part of 1907 and all of 1908, had been slow to develop. Tensions between the white man and the Ute Indians, who dominated the region, still existed in the late nineteenth century. By the time the Dempseys arrived, the area was peaceful, though sparsely populated. Census figures put Colorado's population in 1900 at 539,700.

Uncompahgre seemed to provide a needed scratch for Hyrum Dempsey's itchy feet. The land here was pretty and wild, a place of rocky flats and sagebrush-studded hills. It was a rich range where sugar beets and cattle thrived.

Hyrum found work immediately as a sharecropper. He tended a several-hundred-square-acre area called the Albrush Ranch.

Jack, who was eleven when the family moved to Uncompahgre, found the Albrush a great place to grow up. It was as if he had begun his childhood all over. He rode, fished, and hunted, and became an expert at all. He became a cowboy, too, just like the kind gent he remembered from the Leadville train.

At the Albrush Ranch south of Montrose, Dempsey learned how to ride and rope.

A two-story ranch house came with Hyrum Dempsey's job. Though it sat on a lonely stretch, surrounded only by low barns and cattle pens, the house was a roomy and warm building, a much better accommodation than the huts and tents the Dempseys had been living in. The gypsy days seemed over.

Celia Dempsey loved the new home. From her boardinghouse days in Creede, she was used to a big, busy residence. Using food grown on the Albrush, Mrs. Dempsey cooked enormous meals for her family: stewed chicken and dumplings, yellow butter beans, loaves of salt-rising bread, mutton and veal, kettles of Mexican beans that would last a week.

Life at Uncompahgre for Jack Dempsey meant being outdoors from early morning to late at night. School lasted only about five months of the year. Plowing, reaping and sowing took up the rest of the time. Often the work had an educational side to it. For instance, there were coyotes to trap. Because coyotes regularly crept into the Albrush to kill chickens, lambs, and sheep, Dempsey and his siblings spent many hours trying to catch the critters. Dempsey learned how to set a trap by rubbing the iron with bloody meat to destroy the human scent. He discovered how much gravel to spread around the trap and where to set the trap in the leaves. And he trained himself to always wear gloves or mittens when handling a coyote trap.

When tracking coyotes, Dempsey grasped the need to work upwind and to be patient. He learned to brace himself when he caught an animal in the sights of his big muzzle-loading rifle that had the kick of a cannon.

The Dempsey children and companions such as Rani Kittleson (who later became mayor of Montrose and a lifelong friend), Charley Metcalf, Bill Finnegan, and Les and Frank Campbell discovered how to hunt bees for honey in Uncompahgre. By carefully measuring the time it took a small swarm to reach some raw honey they laid out, the Dempseys and their pals traced the source of the bees and gained a mother lode of rich, wild sweet stuff.

Children around Uncompahgre became adept at treeing bobcats and roping wild burros. Occasionally Dempsey drove a captured burro home and broke it to harness. Dempsey learned to ride so well at Uncompahgre that one summer when his family lived there he went to the county fair in Montrose and talked—unsuccessfully—to a racehorse owner about letting him become a jockey. Jack was still small for his age.

Two kinds of animals that Dempsey took kindly to in Uncompahgre were dogs and rabbits. Dempsey acquired a special brindle bulldog named Denver. Denver possessed a great fighting spirit. In addition, he never cried. For a while Dempsey owned sheep dogs in Uncompahgre, which his family used to herd cattle. Before the Dempseys left Uncompahgre, the dogs, including beloved Denver, were mysteriously poisoned. Denver never cried. But that day Jack did.

When Dempsey would mow hayfields on the ranch, he would often come upon a band of rabbits. Instead of aiming his mower at the tiny creatures, he would swerve around them. Sometimes he would stop the mower completely and, on foot, chase the rabbits away from the machine's blades.

A good part of the labor on the Albrush Ranch involved clearing the land for cattle. Nearly every day Dempsey helped his brothers and father move huge rocks. Dempsey learned how to tie a chain around a boulder and how to rig the chain to a horse or mule. He learned how to use a crowbar and lever to pry loose rocks. And as he learned, he grew. He may have been jockey-sized in those days, but his muscles began to take the definition of a fully developed man.

"I don't ever regret having grown up that way," Dempsey said later. "I was never ill or down with sickness. My body became tough as leather."

Bern Dempsey every now and then dropped in at home during the Uncompahgre years. Bern admired his younger brother's increasing strength. "Wanna Box?" Bern would ask. And the two would box.

Bern by now was Jack's idol. Bern was still taking fights wherever he could find them. In Uncompahgre he resumed coaching his brother. He introduced Jack to the feint, jab and counter. "Bern was a good coach," Dempsey remembered. "As a boxer he had one big problem: a glass chin."

Not only did Dempsey grow strong in Uncompahgre, but he obtained there perhaps his single most important piece of knowledge: resourcefulness. By observing small details on the ranch—the way a bird flapped its wings or how a drop of water stretched out before it fell from a twig—Dempsey gained an acute power of observation. The ability helped him later on as a prizefighter. By closely watching an opponent's footwork, he would figure out, resourcefully, how to shift his defense and attack accordingly. Deciding which stones to step on to cross a stream helped Dempsey understand which moves he should use in a boxing ring.

By forcing himself to remember how to set a trap and how to move a boulder, and by learning to count the number of birds in a flock, Dempsey at Uncompahgre sharpened another resource: his memory. As Kid Blackie and afterward, he remembered when an opponent was about to "telegraph" a punch or when a three-minute round of a fight was about to end. Then he'd move in for the kill.

Finally, in Uncompahgre Dempsey realized the value of practice. For hours he tossed a rope at wild burros. "The way I got better at roping," said Dempsey, "was to do it over and over. Same with boxing. I got better by punching until my arms fell off."

On Saturday nights, most of the residents in the Uncompahgre area, the Dempseys included, went to dances at the Uncompahgre Literary Society (the ULS), a community hall used during the winter for book reviews, debates and spelling bees. Other than Jim Finlen's general store, the ULS was *the* gathering place in the village.

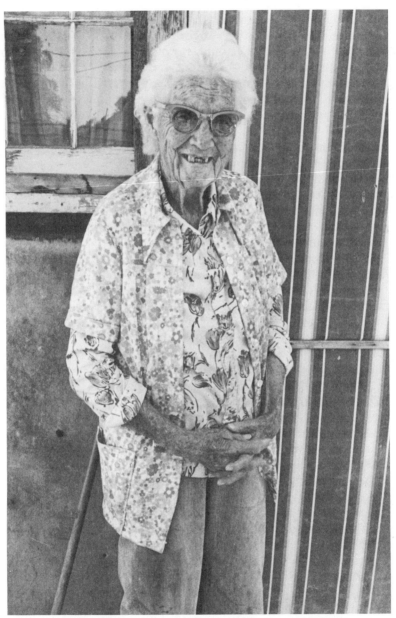

Susie Osborne of Olathe: "Did Jack have a girlfriend? Any one he wanted."

"Those were real nice dances," remembers Susie Osborne, who attended several during the period the Dempseys lived at Uncompahgre. Today, Mrs. Osborne resides in a tiny, screen-porched house in Olathe, Colorado, just north of Montrose. "Did I have a crush on Jack Dempsey?" she responds with a mischievous, gap-toothed grin. "Sure. But I was afraid he'd knock me out. I'm just kidding."

Susie Osborne arrived at the small settlement of Colona, Colorado, six miles down the road from Uncompahgre, the same year the Dempseys came to the Albrush. Susie's father, John M. Pool, had left Springdale, Arkansas, bringing West a wife and eleven children. For the move, John Pool chartered a train car and filled it with his family, five mules and two dozen chickens.

Pool farmed potatoes, corn and hay in Colona. "I started working when I was ten, same as Jack," says Susie Osborne. "I plowed corn. I did what a man did and got nothing." At twelve, she walked seven and one-half miles to downtown Colona to work as a waitress. "I got something for that."

Jack was a happy-go-lucky kid, according to Susie Osborne. The two didn't attend the same school. Dempsey went to a little one-room schoolhouse with the man Susie later married, Pete Osborne. Still, Susie Osborne knew the Dempseys. "Jack's mother was the fighter of the family. She made all them kids toe the mark."

It was at Saturday evening ULS dances—"some went on all night"—that Susie Osborne came to know Dempsey well. "Of course I danced with him. Jack was a good dancer. We did the schottische. You know what that is? It's kind of like the polka. Did Jack have a girl friend? Any one he wanted. Jack was a handsome boy then. When I saw his picture in the paper after he died he was still handsome."

The Dempsey boys, says Mrs. Osborne, knew how to use their fists. Mrs. Osborne recalls one ULS dance in which Bern Dempsey, during an argument over a woman, knocked a man across the room.

Mostly there was music at the ULS dances and not fights. Fiddle, piano or banjo provided the tunes. Pete Osborne played the fiddle, and Susie still has the instrument. It had to be repaired, however. Years back Pete's mother sat on it.

The ULS hall burned down about 1913. Pete Osborne died in 1967 on his fifty-fifth wedding anniversary. For most of their marriage the Osbornes farmed near Montrose. In 1972, Mrs. Osborne moved to Olathe. Pete and Susie were living on a ranch southeast of Montrose in 1919 when Dempsey took the title away from Jess Willard. "Oh, boy," sighs Mrs. Osborne. "That was a good feeling."

Of her memories of Jack Dempsey, Susie Osborne is left with one that still inspires her, gives her goose bumps even. It happened, appropriately perhaps, at the old ULS hall. She and Dempsey were dancing when suddenly Dempsey whispered something to her. "Jack told me he was gonna be boxing champion of the world. I really didn't believe him. I mean, he was just a real country boy in them days."

In spite of the long and arduous hours the Dempseys put in at the Albrush Ranch, the family lost the place. Among small farmers, financial survival demanded meticulous management of land and cattle; and Hyrum Dempsey was no manager.

After a year and a half at the Albrush, the Dempseys fortunately were able to move nearby, to the Masters Ranch, where again they sharecropped. But once more Hyrum couldn't make it work.

When the Dempseys finally had to leave Uncompahgre in late 1908, tears welled up in Celia Dempsey's eyes. The family had been wonderfully happy there. It was a sad day when Mrs. Dempsey took down a sampler, with words by Thomas Carlyle, that hung on the kitchen wall. It read:

MAKE YOURSELF AN HONEST MAN
AND THEN YOU MAY BE SURE
THERE IS ONE LESS RASCAL IN THE WORLD.

Dempsey knew how much his mother believed in their life at Uncompahgre. It hurt him to see her cry for the first time in his life. Ranching was not the only thing that had turned sour in Uncompahgre, Jack guessed. He knew then that his parents' marriage was doomed.

CHAPTER IV

Montrose

"The Jack we knew was peaceable. The Jack who got in that ring was downright vicious."

When the Dempseys lost the second Uncompahgre ranch, Hyrum moved the family north for a year to the community which took its name from Sir Walter Scott's 1819 novel, *The Legend of Montrose.* Originally called Pomona and founded by explorer Joseph Selig in 1882, Montrose was said to have the same rolling hills as the site of a Scottish battle chronicled by Scott.

No Colorado town holds more Jack Dempsey boxing heritage than Montrose. As a young boy, Dempsey experienced in Montrose his first bona fide prizefight. A few years later he returned there to make his professional debut.

In Montrose Dempsey learned to love to fight. In other Colorado places he learned to fight to live.

Seventy-five years ago, Montrose was a cow-town railhead of about fifteen hundred people. It is located not far from the Black Canyon of the Gunnison River, one of the world's foremost wild canyons. The Gunnison River may be nearby, but Montrose and the surrounding area once suffered from a severe lack of water. In 1905, the Denver and Rio Grande (D&RG) Railroad began construction on the Gunnison Tunnel, a six-mile excavation through solid granite that would bring water from the Black Canyon to Gunnison and Delta counties.

Montrose depended on the railroad—not just for water but for nearly everything. The railroad was Montrose's connection to the outside world, its means of shipping the cattle, sugar beets and fruit grown in the area to points across the nation.

The D&RG was looking for men to work on the tunnel when the Dempseys arrived in Montrose in 1909. Hyrum and his older sons immediately enlisted. This time, however, Celia Dempsey decided not to pin all the family's hopes on her husband. Refusing to let the loss of the two ranches drag her down, Celia marched into Montrose and opened the Rio Grande Eating House. Because she had run a boardinghouse in Creede and had fixed meals for eleven children, she felt she could run a restaurant. Besides, no one ever accused Celia Dempsey of being anything less than an excellent cook.

The Rio Grande Eating House, christened with a jug of hard cider, was located on North First Street, close to where the old Montrose railroad station now stands. A ramshackle wooden affair, the restaurant wasn't fancy: a lunch counter, a half dozen tables and a simple kitchen in the back.

The eatery may have been plain, but it quickly gained a reputation for good food among the tunnel workers, railroaders, drifters and cowhands of Montrose. The Rio Grande Eating House's beans were said to be the best in town. And you couldn't beat the restaurant's prices. An all-you-can-eat meal cost twenty-five cents.

Since the restaurant stayed open late, Dempsey, who helped his mother run the place, worked the night shift. He waited on customers, cleared tables, washed dishes and stoked the fire in the dining room stove. When he wasn't busy, he enjoyed going into the kitchen and whipping up for himself a meal big enough to feed three people: steak, ham and eggs, pork chops, and Mexican beans fixed the way his mother taught him. Though still small, Dempsey began to put on weight, thanks to his own home cooking.

At other times when business at the restaurant slowed, Dempsey took a seat at the counter and read the *Police Gazette,* mainly for its boxing news. When customers— mostly males—did come in, Dempsey never tired of watching them and listening to their tales as they played cards, nipped at private whiskey bottles and swore. For Dempsey, the men represented a different breed than the ones he knew in Uncompahgre. These were the type of people he saw frequently in Colorado over the next ten years, and he felt comfortable around them. However, Dempsey stopped short of imitating them. Smoking and drinking, he decided, were habits that would hurt his coordination and stamina in the ring.

When the Rio Grande Eating House didn't require his services, Dempsey hitched a little brown wagon to two dogs and drove the device around Montrose to sell newspapers, including the *Chicago Leader.* He also used the wagon as a means of hauling coal back to the restaurant's stove and as a portable shoeshine parlor on Montrose streets. Occasionally he'd try his luck at mining. On June 14, 1909, Dempsey worked the Torpedo Eclipse Mine near Ouray. To freight ore out of the Eclipse, he checked out a horse that day from the John Ashenfelter Stables in Ouray. The cost? Two dollars.

Though the Dempseys had been like almost everyone else in Uncompahgre—as poor as sandy soil—in Montrose their poverty seemed to stand out. The family, for instance, could not afford to shop by catalog from Sears, Roebuck, as some people in Montrose did, ordering Graphophones, rotary washers, patent leather Blucher shoes or even catarrh cures. The family definitely were have-nots. But unlike what had occurred in Delta, no one in Montrose tried to run the Dempseys out of town. In Montrose, Dempsey started wearing the outfit that he donned for several years hence: a red sweater and tattered gray cap. Only later, when he pulled down million-dollar gates as the heavyweight champion, did he become a natty dresser who favored silk shirts, spats and well-tailored, double-breasted suits.

As a young man, Dempsey paused in Ouray to rent a pack horse.

George Washington Clark, an Abe Lincoln look-alike, served as Dempsey's schoolteacher in Montrose. For the most part, Dempsey got along well with his classmates. There were fights, but not out of anger. For impoverished people like Dempsey, fighting was a way of life. Without a movie theater in Montrose, boxing was the biggest amusement around, for kids as well as for adults. "Everybody worked so hard there," Dempsey said, "that they really looked forward to a good scrap as entertainment."

Two large, male-dominated families lived in the Dempseys' Montrose neighborhood. The Wood clan boasted five boys: Red, Bob, Austin, Brownie and Fred. Austin, a few years older than Dempsey, regularly tussled with Dempsey's older brother Johnny. Jack's younger brother Bruce fought Brownie. And Dempsey took on Fred Wood. It was the first time Dempsey ever fought someone his own age and size. At the time, Dempsey checked in at about 110 pounds.

Down the street from the Dempseys lived the Pitts, a black family whose father was a cook. Joe Dempsey, another of Jack's older brothers, had weekly battles with Hughie Pitts. Johnny boxed Chalky Pitts and Jack squared off with Tommy. One afternoon Dempsey's brothers encouraged Jack to fight Tommy Pitts for a prize. The winner, the Dempsey boys decreed, would receive two chickens. "I won," Dempsey remembered, "though you'd never know it if you'd seen my face."

Now and then Bern Dempsey showed up in Montrose, as he'd done elsewhere, to offer Jack boxing tips. By now Jack's body had begun to fill out. However, Bern said that while bulk would help in the ring, Jack needed speed. Bernie ordered his brother to skip rope in the basement of their Montrose home. For several years thereafter Dempsey never walked down a street; he jumped rope instead. Bernie told his brother to chase horses down Main Street. And he had Dempsey sneak into the racetrack at the county fair to sprint against thoroughbreds. After hours in the restaurant, Bernie would hold out a broomstick and wag it back and forth as quickly as he could. "Hit it, Harry!" Bern would yell. Jabbing and punching, Dempsey often did strike the thin, fast-moving pole.

Just swinging at the broom wasn't enough, Bernie said. Bern showed his brother how to twist the handle around and around to develop stronger wrists and a more powerful grip.

Bern Dempsey had never been a great fighter. A mining accident had sliced off two of his toes and cost him his balance. But Bern had heart. Early in his career, on September 15, 1890, Bern fought and beat the formidable John W. Davis of Red Mountain, Colorado. The bout was held at the Martha Rose Smelter, near Silverton, and it was refereed by Patrick Stanley, the Silverton marshal. Stanley went into the ring with a gun strapped to his leg, as many boxing officials did in those days.

On Saturdays, Dempsey tagged along while Bernie took trips to knockabout saloons in Aspen, Glenwood Springs or closer to home, Ouray. When the food was gone in bars such as the Cabinet, on Ouray's Main Street, the older guys in the place would start drinking. Then the fights would begin, always about 1:00 a.m.

Most of the time the makeshift rings in the saloons were made out of clothesline. The boxing gloves, if available, usually were blood-caked. Yet Dempsey would grab a ringside seat, if the fighters weren't using chairs on each other, and study the styles. He learned a lot watching the barroom fisticuffs, as sloppy as they often became. "I was glad to be there," Dempsey said. "I loved everything about boxing. Watching Bernie made me determined to do well at it."

What Dempsey didn't like about those brawls was witnessing the beatings his brother took. Frequently, Bernie suffered savage poundings about the face.

"I want to fight, like you," said Dempsey, heading back to Montrose after one such thrashing. "But I sure don't want to get busted up so badly."

Bernie had an idea. The next morning he showed his brother, who was twelve at the time, how to toughen his body, something Bernie had neglected to do himself. Bern ordered his brother to chew leatherlike resin from Montrose pine trees. The resin would, Bernie claimed, strengthen the jaw and make it easier to take blows. The stuff tasted horrible, but Dempsey chewed it all day long.

Although some fighters of that period even chewed garlic to make opponents keep their distance, Dempsey never tried that. He liked to fight too much.

Because Bernie had been in fights that were stopped over simple cuts, he urged Jack to apply beef brine to his face and hands to harden them. Regularly, Dempsey went around with bucket in hand to Montrose butchers to collect beef brine. He would then rub the liquid around his eyes. At night, during breaks at the restaurant, he'd soak his hands in the bucket.

Using the pine gum and the brine were two rituals Dempsey kept up after he became heavyweight champion. "Fists of cement," admirers gushed. "Dempsey's head," said Georges Carpentier, the Frenchman who fought Dempsey in a 1921 slugfest and lost, "is the strongest part of his body."

The Gunnison Tunnel, completed by the Bureau of Reclamation, was dedicated by President William Howard Taft on September 23, 1909. A few weeks later the Dempseys left Montrose. Even though his wife's restaurant was doing well, Hyrum Dempsey felt the family could make a better living elsewhere. Provo, Utah, was the Dempseys' next stop. As a family, they never returned to Colorado. Utah became their new home.

Before Jack Dempsey departed Montrose that fall of 1909, he and a couple of friends held a workout in what used to be called the Elephant Corral. The place was actually a fenced area used to break horses. Carl Smith, the boy who had befriended Dempsey in Delta with a toy balloon, remembers seeing Dempsey again as a youngster in Montrose. Smith had traveled to the town with his parents one day in a horse and buggy.

"I happened to pass the Elephant Corral and there he was," Smith says. "He was boxing. Only instead of hitting my balloon, he was beating on a sand bag, I think it was. I was too shy to say hello and Jack was too busy to notice me."

In 1911, Dempsey graduated from the eighth grade in Provo. He had now lived in Utah almost two years. During one of those years, 1910, Halley's comet soared across the skies of the western United States.

After graduation Dempsey returned to Montrose with $1.50 in his pocket and a dream: to become a success and leave poverty behind. Boxing, he felt, was the way to accomplish that dream, to get people to notice him, the same way they noticed Halley's comet.

Several months before, Dempsey had followed by radio from Provo heavyweight Jack Johnson's victory over Jim Jeffries in Reno. After that title fight, Dempsey vowed to be like Jack Johnson in the ring: big, strong and fast. That promise would sustain him through the dark periods ahead.

The year 1911 stands out for two reasons, both only tangentially related to Jack Dempsey. The infamous Alferd Packer died that year. Back in 1874, Packer, then a prospector, had killed and cannibalized five companions near Lake City, Colorado, about fifty miles southeast of Montrose. And also in 1911, brutal floods buried many southern Colorado communities, including Dempsey's hometown of Manassa.

Dempsey had already inched toward his dream by 1911. Physically he was bigger than ever; he now weighed 145 pounds. He also had a new name—two of them, in fact.

Ever since they had lived in Manassa, most of Dempsey's family had called him "Harry." In Utah, just prior to returning to Colorado, Dempsey took the first name of "Jack," after the famous middleweight fighter of the century before, Jack Dempsey, "The Nonpareil." That Dempsey, no relation, fought between 1883 and 1895 and died in Portland at the age of thirty-three.

Coincidentally, Bernie Dempsey had also used the name "Jack Dempsey" when fighting. In fact, any fighter during that time whose name was Dempsey wanted to be called "Jack" because it made him sound as good and as tough as the original Nonpareil, who overpowered every man he fought. Even Johnny Dempsey, another of Jack's older brothers and a sometime lightweight, billed himself as "Jack Dempsey."

If three Jack Dempseys in one family seemed like a lot, Jack still wanted the name.

"Why don't you take a ring name?" brother Bernie said. "You know, 'Kid' somebody or other." During that era "Kid" was a commonly used moniker for boxers. Kid Rowley, Kid Dawson and Kid McCoy were well-known

Western fighters.

After studying his brother's dark complexion and hair, Bernie suggested "Kid Blackie," and the name stuck. Deep down, however, Kid Blackie knew who he was: Jack Dempsey.

After finishing school in Utah, Dempsey considered several destinations: Salt Lake City, Los Angeles, San Francisco. But he felt if he really wanted to fight and make good on his dream, he should return to Montrose, a town that had been receptive to him and to boxing.

So, in early June of 1911, Dempsey hopped a railroad car alone and headed east. He was fifteen, beetle-browed and crew cut. Long, taut muscles covered his slender body.

Things were not easy in Montrose. Dempsey managed to land a job picking fruit at the John Ashenfelter orchard, four miles west of town. Years later, Damon Runyon wrote in a newspaper story, "Jack is the only peach-snatching pugilistic prospect the ring has ever had."

Other jobs followed. Dempsey dug ditches, tossed sacks of sugar beets onto railroad cars, shoveled manure and pitched circus tents. In his spare moments he thought about boxing.

Irvin H. Hanes, a former Montrose resident who later moved to Denver, remembered helping Dempsey in 1911. Hanes' wife, Martha, had lived in Manassa when the Dempseys did. "We invited Jack to live at our house in Montrose that summer. Martha and I were going to spend a few weeks in the mountains. During our absence, Jack turned the house into a gymnasium. On our return we found a feather bed hanging from the ceiling. Jack had been using it as a punching bag. He'd also used one of the spreads as a sweat absorber."

Hanes said that his wife was a bit put out by the whole thing, but felt even worse when she spoke of it to Dempsey. "Jack ran from her like a big kid who knows he has done something wrong."

After about six months of earning small but steady wages in Montrose, Dempsey encountered Charley Diehl. Dempsey had known Diehl as a customer at the Rio Grande Eating House. Dempsey remembered that Diehl had an interest in boxing. In fact, Diehl was one of the more knowledgeable athletic buffs in Montrose. A part-time chef and ore freighter, Diehl for a year had studied in Battle Creek, Michigan, at Bernarr MacFadden's Physical Training School. He wanted to become an exercise director. Diehl supplemented his education with instruction in Chicago from such well-known boxers as Freddie Welsh and Jack Davis.

"Do you think I could ever become a champion fighter?" Dempsey inquired of Diehl one day on a Montrose street.

"Of course you can," said Diehl, "if you work hard enough."

Twenty years later, when someone asked Diehl if he'd really said that, Diehl answered, "Sure, I didn't want to discourage the kid."

It took a lot to discourage Jack Dempsey. Indeed, the smallest bit of encouragement made him more determined than ever to succeed. However, if someone laughed at his dream, Dempsey bitterly resented it. Derision only made him redouble his efforts.

Charley Diehl's words sent Dempsey to work: he soaked his face and hands in brine daily. He chewed more pine gum, put in more roadwork. There came a point, however, when Dempsey knew he had to put Kid Blackie to the test—a boxing test.

"Can you get me a fight, Charley?" he asked Diehl. By now it was the summer of 1912 and Jack was seventeen. The Montrose County Fair, the major event of the area, was approaching. Dempsey thought a fight during fair week might draw a crowd. Diehl agreed. The two went to the local Moose Hall to talk to the manager about sponsoring the bout there. The manager, a cautious man, nixed the idea of charging admission. He didn't think it was ethical. Dempsey left the Moose Hall terribly disappointed.

A few days later Dempsey took a horse he'd been loaned to a nearby blacksmith shop to get it shod. The shop, owned jointly by Fred Wood, Dempsey's boyhood friend, and Fred's father, stood at Cascade and Second streets. Inside it Dempsey learned that his old friend Wood had been doing some boxing. In fact, Wood had built up a reputation as a pretty fair country fighter. "The Fighting Blacksmith," he called himself.

"What would you think," asked Dempsey, "of fighting me?"

"I think we'd make some money," said Wood.

Dempsey eyed Wood. Though a bit musclebound from swinging a hammer, Wood was still about the same size—five feet, ten inches and 145 pounds—as Dempsey.

Under the nickname "Kid Blackie," Dempsey earned a reputation as a regional brawler.

Yet Dempsey had a hunch he could beat the blacksmith.

The following day Dempsey and Wood went to the Moose Hall and rented the place themselves. That way *they* could charge admission; the hall would be theirs. After making payment Dempsey said a little prayer to himself asking someone to please show up to see The Fighting Blacksmith versus Kid Blackie.

To build an audience, Dempsey acted as promoter. He acquired a batch of printed tickets and told people around town about the fight. Since the Moose Hall had no ring, Dempsey and Wood built one in the upstairs dance hall. They threw sawdust on the floor and strung a cord around some jerry-built ring posts.

Finally, Dempsey went into training for the fight. A little shed stood behind the blacksmith shop and Fred Wood's father gave Dempsey permission to use it. Dempsey knew he had to develop a harder punch. He felt it would come from boxing in a crouch. He built a cage in the shed the size of a ring but only four feet high. The low ceiling forced Dempsey to stay in a crouch. Hour after hour he shadowboxed, bent over. The position exhausted Dempsey, but it made him, he sensed, harder to hit and able to deliver harder hits.

Occasionally Dempsey sparred with Charley Diehl, who pretended to be Fred Wood. Diehl would move and duck from side to side. Suddenly Diehl would change styles. Dempsey would study the switch just as closely as he had the coyote tracks in Uncompahgre. Then he would compensate.

As the big day approached, rumor circulated that the bout would never take place. The Women's Christian Temperance Union (W.C.T.U.) mounted a protest against the fight. Though Montrose was a wild and woolly town, it was not without a pious element. Dempsey had once watched Carrie Nation troop into the community in 1908. At the time of the Wood fight, prizefighting in many places in Colorado was still illegal except in exhibition form. The sheriff of Montrose, a man by the name of Gill, told the W.C.T.U. and others that he would be present at the fight. "I promise to stop it if things get out of hand," said Gill.

On fight night Dempsey's nerves jumped like a pea on a snare drum. This was, after all, the biggest contest of his young career. And at twenty-five cents a ticket, it was his professional debut. He and Wood had agreed to split the proceeds. Dempsey hoped there would be proceeds since he had gone into debt to rent the hall. But Dempsey was fighting less for the money than to prove something. He knew many people in Montrose and he wanted them to see his progress as a boxer.

As the audience entered the Moose Hall, Dempsey handed out tickets and stuffed change and bills into his trousers. When it was time to fight, he took off his pants and hung them where he could see them while he fought: on a post along the ring apron.

Underneath, Dempsey wore a faded pair of green silk trunks given to him by Charley Diehl. Diehl had acquired the trunks from Freddie Welsh in Chicago. Diehl also lent Dempsey a pair of cracked but serviceable boxing gloves.

Charley Diehl agreed to announce the fight. His cousin Morris served as referee. Nels Carlson, a Ridgway, Colorado, gambler, horse racer and sometime fighter known as "The Swede Kid" took a seat at ringside. He would be the timekeeper.

Charley Diehl also acted as Dempsey's second: he'd hold a water pail and handle the mouth sponge. Years later, Diehl, who still owned the boxing gloves from that fight, said he thought Dempsey was in for the biggest licking of his career that night.

Dempsey and Wood went at it from the opening bell. Each wanted a quick knockout. But they were too evenly matched physically for that to happen.

Round one ended even. In round two, Wood charged and Dempsey struck him on the chin. Wood slumped to the sawdust. He got up slowly, but Dempsey was not experienced enough to finish him off. Instead, he let Wood recover before resuming.

An overconfident Dempsey got caught by a Wood punch to the stomach in round three. Doubling over from the pain and gasping for breath, Dempsey seemed near defeat. However, Wood, as Dempsey had done to him the round before, simply stood there and watched.

The hours of roadwork and flailing at the broomstick, coupled with the days of working in a crouch, gave Dempsey a sudden rush of energy. From somewhere deep inside he gained a second wind and attacked Wood. Acting like a wild man, Dempsey lashed at his friend with a flurry of punches. A haymaker to Wood's cheek sent The Fighting Blacksmith to the floor face first. Dempsey, dazed from the blow to his belly, later did not even remember taking the big sidearm swing.

Dempsey stared in horror at a lifeless Wood. "Honest to God, sheriff," Dempsey protested hoarsely, "I didn't know I hit him that hard!"

Though the crowd cheered Kid Blackie, Dempsey did not smile. He grabbed Charley Diehl's pail of water and dumped it on his opponent. Eventually Wood regained consciousness.

"Let's fight some more," Wood said groggily. But Dempsey had had enough.

After the fight Dempsey checked his pants pocket. The gate receipts came to forty dollars. He split the cash with Wood. Then the two friends pushed the chairs back to make room in the Moose Hall for a fiddling contest.

The Wood bout made Dempsey realize he could fight, even box a little. "I knew I had to improve, but I was happy by what happened."

Susie Osborne, Dempsey's dance partner from Uncompahgre days, did not witness the Wood battle. However, Susie's husband, Pete, did. The fight, in fact, took place during the couple's honeymoon. Pete Osborne, says his widow, was not particularly interested in boxing, only in Jack Dempsey. And the Jack Dempsey that Osborne saw that summer night in 1912 was a stranger.

"The Jack we knew was peaceable," says Susie. "The Jack who got in that ring was downright vicious."

Almost thirty years after that fight, Charles E. Adams, editor of the Montrose *Daily Press*, wrote the following of Dempsey's success:

> All of which shows you that no one can tell how far that little dirty-faced boy you may see on the street, flattening his nose against the windows looking at toys, is going to go when he grows into manhood.

Dempsey remained in Montrose after the Fred Wood fight, taking jobs where he could find them. Periodically, he left town for Telluride, Colorado, southwest of Montrose, to take seasonal labor and work in the gold mines there when possible. Dempsey's next big fight, however, also took place in Montrose. This time he faced Andy Malloy, a journeyman middleweight twelve years Dempsey's senior.

Malloy was not really a stranger. Dempsey had known him in Creede as Bernie's occasional adversary.

Again Dempsey decided to rent the Montrose Moose Hall. The fight was scheduled to take place late in 1912. Shortly before the bout, however, the Moose Hall manager canceled. "A dance has been set for that evening," he told Dempsey. "I don't want the floor messed up this time."

That evening, upon noticing that more people attended the dance than his fight with Fred Wood, Dempsey went out of the fight-promoting business and nearly quit boxing. "What's the use?" he told a friend. "Nobody wants to see me." However, a week later the Moose manager relented and said there could be a fight on a non-dance night.

That bout took place, but not without a hitch. C.J. Moynihan, then mayor of Montrose, and George Alford, the town's night marshal, heard that the Kid Blackie-Andy Malloy bout might be fixed. An hour before the fight the two city officials went to the Moose Hall. Moynihan told Alford to seize and hold the attendance receipts until the fight was over.

"Why?" asked a stunned Dempsey.

"If the fight's on the level," said Moynihan, "you'll get your money. If the fight's crooked, the dough'll be returned to the spectators."

Dempsey and Malloy looked at each other for a moment, then nodded.

From the opening bell Dempsey realized how far over his head he was. Andy Malloy was a skilled boxer. He hit Dempsey as he pleased. Malloy left no opening for Dempsey to slip in and land a punch.

For two rounds Malloy pummeled Dempsey. If Malloy had packed a heavier punch Dempsey would have been knocked out. In fact, Malloy, noticing an edge, eased up. Still, at the end of round two, Dempsey hobbled to his corner, his knees shaky. The crowd started to leave, believing the fight over. Moynihan wondered if maybe the fight *was* rigged. Malloy was that far ahead on points.

During the rest period before round three, however, Dempsey felt the same surge of power, the same second wind that he'd discovered in the Wood bout. When the bell rang to start the third round, Dempsey went after Malloy with all he had. Here is how Mayor Moynihan recalled it: "Dempsey left his corner with the speed and ferocity of a hyena, and before Malloy could protect himself, delivered one of those punishing blows for which he afterwards became famous."

The punch, similar to the one that had decked Fred Wood, sent Malloy crashing to the floor. Dempsey had won by another knockout.

Shortly after the fight, this editorial appeared in the Montrose *Daily Press:*

We have paid our respects from time to time to the so-called "boxing exhibitions" used as the dignified title of the "prize fight." The point we are trying to emphasize is the manner in which the title is used for the purpose of pulling the wool over the eyes of the law.

There was an exhibition of this kind the other night and much stress placed on the claim for it that it was simply an artistic exhibition of manly art. It was announced beforehand that it was not to be a "knockout," but simply a ten-round sparring match.

The affair ended with one of the particulars cuddled up on the platform writhing in agony and wailing, "I'm all in, boys."

If this wasn't a prize fight we are wondering what a prize fight is. The beating around the bush makes us weary. The average "boxing exhibition" is nothing but a prize fight and should be treated as such.

For Jack Dempsey, a boxing exhibition or a prizefight meant the same thing: a way to make a name and some money. The dream was taking shape.

CHAPTER V

Telluride

"The best friends I ever had."

Dempsey bounced like a BB in a boxcar from one Colorado town to another during 1913. Not only was he looking for employment, but for an opportunity to box. During this time he acquired a number of acquaintances. It's unlikely, however, that any people Dempsey met during this period made as great an impression on him as two brothers from Telluride named Andy and Pat Malloy.

Although the Malloys showed Dempsey a great deal about boxing, what he gained from the brothers were things Dempsey needed during his footloose, struggle-filled, and at times lonely youth: loyal friendships and strong encouragement.

Of all the Colorado communities Dempsey hopscotched, Telluride, with its grand cliffs, velvet meadows and bucolic stillness, was certainly the most stunning. Yet the scenery did not bring Dempsey to Telluride. He came to make a living and to better himself as a boxer. The Malloys would help him do both.

Dempsey first arrived in Telluride in late 1912 when he was a mature seventeen-year-old. The town then had approximately five thousand residents. Dempsey lived in Telluride off and on for a year and a half, hopping a freight and leaving temporarily whenever word came of a higher-paying job or a promising fight. Usually his destination was another Colorado mining camp where jobs were more plentiful, and where residents appreciated a rock-'em, sock-'em saloon brawl, and where the law looked the other way or simply didn't exist.

In those camps Dempsey polished his boxing skills and his acting. Wearing his familiar red sweater and cap, Dempsey would hitch up his pants, stride into a tavern and announce brazenly, in his best John L. Sullivan voice, "I can't sing, I can't dance, but I'll lick anyone in the house!"

And he *would* fight anyone—for a buck. Through part of 1912 and all of 1913 and 1914, Dempsey had more than one hundred spur-of-the-moment clashes. There is little mention of them anywhere except what Dempsey and a few other people passed along.

Some of Dempsey's saloon opponents during those years outweighed him by more than 100 pounds. The match-ups often made the crowds howl with laughter, for Dempsey weighed less than 150 pounds and had a high-pitched voice and a half-shaved head. But he was serious. Against bigger men, Dempsey always tried to end the fight quickly, swinging swiftly inside, usually straight up, aiming for the jaw. The fights he lost were rare. When he did lose, he just tried harder the next time.

Cyril Cummins, a power plant worker from Farmington, New Mexico, remembers a story that his father, Cyril Sr., told often. It seems that Cyril Sr. once got into a bar fight with Dempsey in Rico, Colorado, and won. "Many years later," says the younger Cummins, "Jack Dempsey sent my father a pair of tickets to one of his big fights. That defeat had meant a lot to him, I guess."

In time Dempsey developed a routine with small-town bartenders. Just about every mining camp saloon in those days had a free-lunch counter. Dempsey would hang around the counter for an hour or so, filling his empty stomach; then the bartender would try to throw him out. The scenario would go something like this:

DEMPSEY: OK, I'll leave. But hey, would you like to be a matchmaker? Get me a fight here and you can keep half the profits.

BARKEEP: I don't want any fights in this place.

DEMPSEY: C'mon. I'll bet you got some guy in here that annoys you and your customers. And I'll bet nobody's ever had the guts to take him on.

BARKEEP: As a matter of fact we do have one fella ....

In nearly every saloon a bully existed. Sometimes the bartender arranged the bout with the troublemaker and sometimes Dempsey just found him on his own. Almost always the bully snickered at Dempsey's slight build and short hair. Listening to Dempsey's girlish voice made the bully smile. "This is going to be easy," the tormentor would bellow. But once in the ring Dempsey fought not like a girl but a man—a man possessed.

"Some of those bullies came at me like mountain lions," Dempsey said later. "And some of them couldn't have licked my sister. But it didn't matter to me. I took them all on. And it made me better."

If Dempsey faced a crafty fighter in those early fights, he would thrust out his brine-soaked face and take everything the other man had to offer. When his opponent tired, Dempsey would move forward and go for a knockout. If he faced a hitter, he would resort to his Montrose crouch and combine it with speed as a defense.

He realized there was no use slugging it out with, say, a lumberjack who nearly doubled him in size. Dempsey discovered that if he hit a pile-driving bruiser on the chin and the man didn't blink, he'd then go for the stomach. And if he still didn't blink, then Dempsey had a final solution: "I'd run like hell."

Usually at the end of these tank town fights someone passed a hat. The take could often be as much as forty dollars—a nice sum for Dempsey and the bartender to split.

Instead of moving from saloon to saloon in Telluride, Dempsey used the town as a base camp from which to operate. At 8870 feet, Telluride is one of the most remote of Colorado's mining camps. Though separated from Ouray, Colorado, by six mountain miles, Telluride from Ouray by paved road is fifty miles away.

While most of the gold is gone, the mountains around Telluride still yield some lead, zinc and silver. The highest peak, 13,000-foot Ajax, stands sentinel over the Swiss-like village located at the end of a box canyon. Twisting down the craggy face of Ajax is Bridal Veil Falls.

Shortly after landing in Telluride, which at the time was nearing the end of the first of three mining booms, Dempsey met the Malloy brothers. He knew Andy, of course, from their Montrose fight of a few months before. Though Dempsey had licked Andy at that meeting, the loser held no grudge. Andy was glad to see Dempsey again and immediately cultivated a friendship. Pat Malloy, two years younger than Andy, also was a boxer. Both Malloys were mule skinners by trade. Years spent on the Western Slope of the Continental Divide had taught the Malloys how to hold their own, whether hauling ore down a mountain on a mule or standing up to a bruiser in a barroom free-for-all.

Though a hard-bitten twosome, the Malloys decided to look after young Jack Dempsey. Andy showed Dempsey how to pack a mule and how to throw a better jab. Dempsey in turn tried to be a mule skinner. He had, after all, ridden a mule to school on occasion in Uncompahgre. But he found handling a team of eight mules to be a lot more difficult than it looked.

More than likely the Malloy brothers, rowdy, fun-loving bachelors, introduced Dempsey to some of the mysteries of the opposite sex. Andy Malloy certainly had experience with women. He was a carouser of the first order. One Telluride old-timer remembered Malloy staying out in the town's dance halls until 4:00 a.m., then heading toward the mines with a team of mules two hours later.

The Malloys held the record for loading out a string of mules with 100-pound bags of ore. Rumor had it that Andy, paunchy and balding but tough as tree bark, had knocked down a stubborn mule with a bare fist. A 160-pounder, Andy had fought all over southern and central Colorado—from Saguache to Pagosa Springs to South Platte. Most of his fights were pickup bouts, but occasionally he competed in organized contests better known as "exhibitions." Andy had victories over Grand Junction's Kid West and a hard-rock miner from Leadville known as "Gilpin Red." In 1903, Andy had gone twenty rounds with Fireman Jim Flynn before getting knocked out. Flynn was a Pueblo fighter with a national reputation.

Andy Malloy laid claim to the Rocky Mountain light heavyweight title. However, ownership of that crown was open to dispute. No one knew of any other light heavyweights.

Pat Malloy was a good fighter, too, though not quite as talented as his brother. Pat also had tangled with Jim Flynn. In 1901, Flynn flattened Pat in six rounds.

What both Malloys gave Dempsey was confidence. Sensing Dempsey's dream, the brothers told their young friend, as Charley Diehl had done in Montrose, that if he worked hard he could become a champion boxer.

The Malloys shared lodgings with Dempsey and lent him

Andy Malloy and Dempsey, here in Telluride, engaged in numerous ring encounters across Colorado.

food and money. But most of all, by being with him, by inspiring him during some lean times, the brothers served to remind Dempsey that his dream was within reach.

Dempsey, with the Malloys' help, gained a job at Telluride's Smuggler-Union Mine. When he wasn't mining, Dempsey trained in a ring the Malloys had built at Telluride's Davis Park on the southeastern edge of town.

"Look for a man's goods and bads," Pat Malloy stressed during training sessions at Davis Park. "Find out if he's a boxer or a puncher. No fighter has everything. If his chin is pure concrete, the belly may be jelly. And just the reverse. If he boxes well, he probably can't punch. If he has a great punch, he probably can't box."

Late in the spring of 1913, Andy Malloy talked Dempsey into a rematch. It would be Kid Blackie versus the Rocky Mountain champ once more, only this time at Telluride's Davis Park.

Charley Diehl agreed to come down from Montrose to serve as referee. Each boxer, Diehl declared, would wear six-ounce gloves. The fight would go twenty rounds, a standard number in many bouts in those days. A knockdown was considered one round and contestants rested three minutes, then continued fighting.

The Davis Park audience, mostly miners, came to the bout to witness blood. "Malloy will kill that damn kid," someone yelled.

Dempsey stood poker-faced in his corner before the opening bell. His only sign of nerves was the way he worked his taped hands deeper into his small gloves. Even though he had once beaten Malloy, Dempsey was not supposed to last more than ten rounds this time. While not as quick as his younger opponent, Malloy was a wily veteran who, most believed, had lost in Montrose by a fluke.

The Telluride fight proved a bewildering surprise. Both men hit the canvas a half dozen times. In the nineteenth round, Malloy, arm weary and badly beaten about the head and ribs, looked over at the referee. "Charley!" Malloy groaned. "I've had it!"

To the crowd's astonishment, Dempsey recorded an upset. Diehl clasped the bloodied young miner's left hand and raised it. "I declare Kid Blackie the winner!" Diehl shouted.

Then a fan hollered, "What's the kid's *real* name?"

"Dempsey!" answered Diehl with a smile. "I declare Jack Dempsey the winner!"

Later, Malloy came up to Dempsey and put his arm around him. "Jack," said the old mule skinner, "you're too good to be traveling by yourself. Why don't you let me be your manager?"

Dempsey agreed. And Malloy, as many others would do in the years to come, became Dempsey's manager: his first manager. The two teamed up periodically as manager and fighter over the next few years. Malloy even wrote away for fights. He got one via mail for Dempsey in 1915 in Salt Lake City against Jack Downey. When Malloy and Dempsey finally split up, it was not over a difference in opinion. Rather, it was because Malloy could no longer obtain fights for Dempsey. No one could.

———

When the mining slowed and when Malloy couldn't find competition for his young charge, Dempsey washed dishes in Telluride at a bordello run by a popular madam known as "Big Billy." Though it would have been natural for Dempsey to be Big Billy's bouncer, he did not have that job. In truth, Dempsey never worked as a bouncer, despite stories to the contrary.

But he did work at Big Billy's. Today, that establishment is a restaurant called The Senate. Three quarters of a century ago, however, the building was a boisterous hangout where a customer once blew off a sheriff's ear and where two companions, after a drinking binge, decided to shoot one another.

Make no mistake: the Telluride that Jack Dempsey knew was about as polite as a stevedore's locker room. In Dempsey's time, the town, referred to as "the City of Gold," boasted twenty-six saloons and more than one hundred prostitutes, or "sporting ladies." Pacific Avenue, also called "Popcorn Alley" and located just a block below Telluride's main street (Colorado Avenue), featured rows of sporting houses run by madams named Diamond Tooth Leona and Jew Fanny. On payday, Popcorn Alley bars such as the Pick and Gad, the Gold Belt, and the Silver Bell turned into snap-crackling dens of potential trouble.

The bars, brothels, dancehalls and gaming parlors in Telluride never closed in those days. Telluride was a lusty, prosperous, hell-raising corner of Colorado. Men grew rich overnight there. Others died without a dime. It all depended on one's luck, both at the mines and at the gaming tables. Fortunes were made and lost at the turn of a roulette wheel.

No one counted on the law much in Telluride. Butch Cassidy allegedly robbed his first bank in Telluride while the local sheriff slept. Occasionally a Telluride policeman woke up long enough to toss a bandit into the town jail, which stood across the street from Big Billy's.

When gold mining ceased in the 1920s, Telluride fell on some hard times. Three-hundred miles of tunnels closed and dozens of miners' shacks that dotted the hillsides went abandoned. Bootleggers came to town for a while in the late 1920s. In 1929, an "honest" bank president in Telluride named Charles Waggoner, sympathetic to the miners' unemployment woes, swindled $500,000 from a New York City bank to help them. Waggoner was quickly caught and imprisoned.

A brief mining resurgence took place in Telluride in the 1930s, then nothing for the next thirty years. In the 1960s,

Laboring in Colorado's mines provided Dempsey with muscle and money.

hippies opened the boarded-up miners' shacks and moved in. In 1969, white gold was discovered in Telluride. Snow that had buried the town each winter suddenly became the community's salvation. Some of America's best skiing conditions caused Telluride to rebound. Big Billy's became The Senate and earned kudos as one of the finest restaurants in the Rockies. The Senate's circa-1880 wooden bar, a counter that Jack Dempsey surely leaned on, was restored, as were spittoons and several pieces of Victorian-era furniture. Other sturdy brick buildings in town also were reclaimed, including the Sheridan Opera House, which still bears on one wall this Dempsey-era message: "OPERA HOUSE PICTURE SHOW every evening—admission ten cents and 15 cents."

Today, Telluride is a town-that-time-forgot tourist center wedged in the awesome San Miguel Valley. While the community of eleven hundred residents tries to hang on to the Western flavor that Jack Dempsey knew, that is not always easy. Annual film, jazz and bluegrass music festivals lure thousands of visitors each year. Telluride's great skiing is no longer a well-kept secret. Additional vacationers flock to Telluride for hiking, fishing in the San Miguel River, and roller-coaster jeep rides. A one-billion-dollar satellite village, with glittering condominiums, fashionable boutiques and additional chairlifts, is planned.

In the wake of Telluride's enormous progress, only a handful of Jack Dempsey memories remain. Any old-timer who might have a recollection of Dempsey has either died or been run off by the great influx of newcomers. The only Telluride resident who can say much about young Dempsey is Arlene Reid. A Kansan originally, Mrs. Reid came to Telluride in 1937 to work as a nurse at the old miners' hospital. Two years after that institution shut its doors in 1964, the building, located hard against the mountains on the north side of town, became a museum operated by the San Miguel County Historical Society.

A warren of rooms holding antiquated mining tools and dusty Western memorabilia, the Telluride museum is Arlene Reid's life. She can talk for hours about a rusty, complicated-looking mining pump.

Mrs. Reid can talk of photographs, too, including one significant old black-and-white shot featuring Jack Dempsey. Hanging on an obscure first-floor wall of the museum, the picture shows Dempsey sparring with Pat Malloy at Davis Park.

The Davis Park ring, Mrs. Reid reports, was torn down long ago. The field where it stood now is used for baseball games and as a landing strip for hang gliders. "I always thought," says Arlene Reid, fingering a corner of the photograph, "that Davis Park ought to be declared a historic site." Telluride is, in fact, listed as a National Historic Landmark.

Mrs. Reid explains that Andy Malloy finally moved to Montana where he married his childhood sweetheart and then died of silicosis, or "miner's tuberculosis." (Silicosis, the fate of many who worked Colorado's mining camps in the early years, also claimed Bern Dempsey in 1935.) Pat Malloy stayed on in Telluride until the Great Depression shut down the mines for the last time. Then he, like so many Telluride folk, departed for parts unknown.

Arlene Reid never met Jack Dempsey. "I wish I had known him," she says, rearranging some photo albums on an end table. "A big, strapping kid. He sounded very likeable." Then with a shy smile: "Of course, I'm not sure we would have had much in common."

Through the years Mrs. Reid has met a number of museum visitors who *have* known Dempsey. "One man came through a few years ago and said he knew Dempsey back in the early days in Telluride. He'd heard Dempsey was sick in New York and he was going to visit him there before Jack died."

Another visitor, according to Mrs. Reid, did just the opposite. He came to Telluride from New York after visiting Dempsey at his Broadway restaurant. Dempsey talked to that visitor about Telluride.

"Those two mule skinner brothers," Dempsey said to the visitor, his eyes glistening partly by infirmities and partly by the memory, "were the best friends I ever had."

CHAPTER VI

Cripple Creek

"Far as I know, Dempsey never turned down poor old George."

Of the many fights Jack Dempsey had during his Colorado days, none taxed him more, both physically and mentally, than the seven rounds he spent with George Coplen in Cripple Creek in the spring of 1913.

Located ten miles southwest of Pikes Peak, Cripple Creek once boasted a population of 35,000. Now it has perhaps 800. Although a Kentucky-born prospector named Crazy Bob Womack struck gold in Cripple Creek in 1878, the rush didn't start until a decade later; nobody had believed Crazy Bob. When things did get roaring in Cripple, the district became known as "the World's Greatest Gold Camp." In 1899, $59 million in gold was pulled from the district, an area which included several outlying towns. At one point, three railroads and two trolley car systems rumbled through the district. Each day, more than a dozen trains passed by, hauling gold ore, miners and visitors.

Cripple Creek's biggest boom took place around the turn of the century. With the great influx of gold miners came women of the evening who set up fancy bawdy houses along Myers Avenue, a five-hundred-yard stretch of sin. Pearl DeVere, with a taste for the Parisian, opened one of the most glittering pleasure palaces in Cripple's glittery red-light neighborhood. The town also featured the requisite mining camp gaming parlors and a famous bistro, among many, called the Bucket of Blood.

Cripple Creek gathered special footnotes in history as it grew. In 1895 the only bullfight ever staged in the United States took place nearby. Groucho Marx once drove a grocery wagon in Cripple. And Texas Guinan, later a famed speakeasy proprietress in New York City, played the organ at an area church.

Though there still is an occasional flurry of gold mining, or at least talk of drilling, the last regularly working mine shaft in Cripple ceased operations in the early 1960s. The closing came when the price of gold froze and production costs soared.

Today, Cripple Creek, which supposedly gained its name more than one hundred years ago through a series of bungled happenings—a log fell on one man, his friend shot himself in the hand and their cow broke its leg—is a busy summertime tourist site of boutiques, ice cream parlors, a museum and a narrow-gauge railroad that runs to Victor, seven miles south. Nearby is the popular Mollie Kathleen Mine. The Mollie Kathleen is still open, though only to sightseers.

Jack Dempsey came to Cripple in 1913 from Telluride to work in the mines and try to pick up a fight. Dempsey quickly got a job at the Mollie Kathleen. He also got picked on.

Bern Dempsey, who had worked the Golden Cycle Mine in Cripple Creek for a while, urged his brother to come to the gold camp. At first Dempsey was known in town as Bern's kid brother. One day after Dempsey had been in Cripple for a few weeks, the camp bully stopped to watch him shovel ore. The bully leered at Dempsey and then threw dirt on him. When it happened again, Dempsey asked the miner, who weighed more than two hundred pounds, to stop.

"What'll you do if I don't?" the ruffian replied, still grinning.

"Leave me alone or else," Dempsey said.

More dirt followed. Suddenly Dempsey leaped out of his pit and went after the taunting miner. A right cross to the man's nose sent the bully flying. When word spread that Bern's kid brother had coldcocked the district lout, everyone wanted to see Dempsey and say thanks.

At one point Dempsey and his brother took out a lease on a Cripple Creek mine. They promised the owner twenty-five percent if and when they struck ore. Digging without help, machinery or any safety equipment, the Dempsey brothers tried to make the mine work, but they couldn't.

As with most mining camps where there was an abundance of males, boxing had a rich history in Cripple Creek. In the late 1890s, fighters such as Dynamite Dick and Giant Powder George used to tangle for beer in the bars. In 1902, Jack Johnson, then a janitor at a dive in Cripple

Creek's Poverty Gulch and later the heavyweight champion of the world, fought Mexican Pete Everett in Cripple in a bout that lasted twenty rounds. Tom "Sailor Boy" Sharkey, who once fought for the heavyweight title, also took on Mexican Pete in town. Bernard Baruch, later a financial genius and advisor to presidents, once mined at Cripple's Bull Hill and fought on the side. In one bout Baruch squared off with the champion of Altman, a suburban camp, and beat the man in two rounds in a fight held underground and illuminated by candlelight.

During the Johnson-Jeffries heavyweight bout of 1910—the fight that Dempsey heard by radio in Utah—officials at the Western Union office in Cripple Creek posted the results, round by round, on a board at the Branch Billiard Hall. A large and enthusiastic crowd stood by the board till the end.

Even in the 1930s, when Cripple Creek had seen its glory days, the community continued to support boxing. During the Depression, a clever fighter named Dutch Messer came out of Cripple Creek. A hunchback, when Messer shrugged his shoulders in the ring he presented an extremely difficult target to hit.

In May, 1913, Bern Dempsey, though pushing forty, signed to fight George Coplen, "the Great White Hope of Cripple Creek." Coplen, a lanky, rawboned veteran, had once sparred with Jack Johnson. Upon learning this, and not wanting to embarrass himself in front of his fellow miners, Bern Dempsey decided to back out of the fight. He wired his brother Jack, who was in West Virginia with their father on another brief, ill-fated, get-rich-quick scheme.

"Got you fight," the wire said. "Come quick."

When Dempsey arrived in Cripple Creek, following three days of riding freight trains, his brother told him, "You gotta take my place."

"What's this guy Coplen like?" Dempsey asked.

"He's done some boxing," said Bern, "but he's an ore shoveler. Harry, I don't want to fight him."

"Aw, c'mon," said Dempsey. "Anybody can flatten him."

"Then you flatten him," said Bernie.

Earlier, Bernie had taken a fifty-dollar guarantee from the fight's promoter and had already spent it.

Dempsey, never one to turn down a fight, agreed to stand in for his brother. But the long rail journey and Cripple Creek's nearly two-mile-high altitude, tired him. He wanted to rest. Bernie, however, wanted him to train. He even urged his brother to drop the name "Kid Blackie" for the fight.

"Call yourself 'Jack Dempsey'," Bernie said. That was the name Bern originally had registered under to fight Coplen.

No one told the fight's promoter of the last-minute change. "I'm going to stop this fight!" the promoter cried angrily when he learned of the substitution. George Coplen, who weighed 165 pounds to Dempsey's 145, also considered stopping the fight before it started. "I might kill this kid," Coplen said to the promoter after Dempsey shed a borrowed bathrobe to reveal a wiry frame.

An all-male audience jammed the Lyric Opera House that

Souvenirs from the Dempsey/Coplen bout wound up in the Cripple Creek Museum.

cool night in 1913. Women were not allowed in. Many men considered it bad luck to let females view a boxing match.

When the referee introduced Jack Dempsey—a gawky youth instead of a tough old hand as the crowd expected—the Lyric erupted with a chorus of boos.

"Look," Dempsey said to the promoter, who hovered near the ring. "That guy's a two-to-one favorite. If I were you I'd bet on me. Do it and then split the money with me."

The promoter eyed Dempsey curiously. Finally he signaled for the fight to begin.

Dempsey dropped Coplen six times in round one. But each time the Cripple Creek native got up and came back for more. In round two, Coplen went down only twice and began to look stronger. In fact, during the early part of the second round Coplen nearly stopped the fight after connecting a roundhouse with Dempsey's ear. Later, Dempsey would say of that blow, "For a second I thought the building had blown up under my feet."

By round three, the thin air of Cripple Creek had caught up with Dempsey. He was having trouble breathing. Coplen's stamina was not much better. The fight continued for three more rounds with each fighter somehow staggering onward. At the end of round six Dempsey slumped onto a stool in his corner. His eyes were glazed and his chest was pumping like a steam engine at full throttle.

"I quit!" he gasped.

"You can't quit!" Bern shouted. "You gotta win if we're gonna get anything!" Then Bernie pushed his brother forward into the ring.

Dempsey leveled Coplen twice more in round seven. Each time, however, the Cripple Creek boxer somehow righted himself. Drawing on an inner strength that he'd come to know well, Dempsey turned on Coplen with a tumult of exhausted swings. One caught the older fighter on the jaw and toppled him for a third time in the round. As he began to rise, Coplen clutched the rope for support. Dempsey, his own legs feeling like Jell-O, his face and chest bloody, looked at the referee.

"Can't you do something?" Dempsey sputtered.

With that, the referee went over to Dempsey and held his arm in the air. The fight had been stopped, a rare event in those days. Kid Blackie, aka Jack Dempsey, had won on a technical knockout.

Several factors kept Dempsey on his feet that evening.

One, he loved the applause. A group of appreciative spectators always made Dempsey try harder. Endurance, built through months of preparation, also helped him. And so did resourcefulness. By calling the referee's attention to Coplen's condition, Dempsey aided his own cause.

"What I learned from that fight," Dempsey said, "was that not all fights are won with fists."

The Coplen fight not only was one of the hardest for Dempsey, but it was one of his most disappointing. After the bout Dempsey and Bern went to the promoter's office around the corner from the Lyric Opera House. There they expected to collect money from bets Jack had told the promoter to make.

"I didn't place any bets," the promoter said nastily. "And even if I did I wouldn't give you anything." He pointed to Dempsey. "You weren't even supposed to be in the fight tonight."

For all his efforts Dempsey wound up penniless.

Years later a rumor circulated through Cripple Creek that Dempsey and Coplen had fought for the hand of Georgia-Belle, a beautiful madam at Mikado's on Myers Avenue. The story bore no truth. Dempsey fought for the experience, the thrill and the money. And when he didn't earn a cent, it depressed him enormously. "I don't ever remember being so down as after that fight," he said.

The Coplen bout became part of a familiar pattern for Dempsey. When he wasn't being cheated out of winnings, he couldn't get fights. And when he got an infrequent fight, someone took his money.

Bern Dempsey returned to the mines after the fight. His brother walked twenty-five miles over the mountains to Canon City, Colorado. There, Dempsey grabbed a freight train to Telluride. The trip was a long one. It gave the young boxer plenty of time to reflect on the sad state of his dream.

Though Francis Gunn never saw Jack Dempsey fight, many times he watched the man who almost ended Dempsey's career.

In a rambling yellow house up a bumpy road a few blocks

Cripple Creek's George Coplen tested Dempsey's endurance in a memorable 1913 contest.

west of Bennett Avenue, Cripple Creek's main artery, lives the pleasant little man who knew the late George Coplen well.

A jolly soul with a perfectly round head and a penchant for bolo neckties, Gunn was born on Crystal Street in Cripple Creek on January, 14, 1904. Gold had lured his father from Detroit.

"It took two camp doctors to deliver me," Gunn says, clasping and unclasping his hands while sitting at his kitchen table. "I guess they needed two doctors. I weighed thirteen-and-a-half pounds."

Music and mining vied for Gunn's attention as a youth. His parents encouraged piano studies, which took him to California as a teenager. Then he returned to Colorado abruptly. "I had to prove to myself that I could be a miner," Gunn says. When the Isabella Mine, where his father was superintendent, burned in 1919, Gunn came home to go to work. Then it was back to California again, this time to do odd jobs. Then off to the Yukon to seek his fortune. Then back to Cripple for most of his adult life.

As a Cripple Creek youngster, Gunn used to box at the town fire station. Franklin Ferguson, owner of the Mollie Kathleen, promoted fights at the firehouse. "I was pretty fair," Gunn reports.

What about George Coplen? "George used to live up the block from me. He was a long, tall guy. He used to keep his hands in his pockets all the time. My mother called him 'Highpockets.' As a boxer, George was a ham 'n egger. Wild."

Coplen worked the district mines as a young man. Someone there told him he had the build of John L. Sullivan, the fighter Dempsey's mother so admired. The compliment drove Coplen to devote more than twenty years to boxing.

"My brother Harold, who died a year or so later, went to that Dempsey fight at the Lyric," says Gunn. "I was too young, although I did go to the Lyric many times after that, before it burned down. I was even there the night it burned. Somebody's cigarette, they said. A few weeks before the fire, I saw *Birth of a Nation* at the Lyric.

"Harold told me that the only reason Dempsey won that fight was because he had a fighting heart. I've got to believe it."

Dempsey was also careful, according to Francis Gunn. "A friend of mine, Wilbur Lewis, worked at the Isabella Mine here with Jack. Wilbur said that Jack saw to it he never hurt himself or overdid it while working in the mines. And mining was hard work."

Gunn witnessed many fights in Cripple Creek. On Labor Day, 1922, he saw George Coplen battle Fireman Jim Flynn at the Union Ball Park. "When Flynn came in at the depot the day before the fight," recalls Gunn, "Coplen insulted him. Coplen wanted to fight him right there. When they did fight, Flynn knocked out Coplen in the first round. Oh, my God, the fight was over so quickly. After that Coplen lost to everybody. His career was finished."

George Coplen lived most of his life with his Russian-born mother on the second floor of a house on Cripple's Welty Block. "Poor old George," says Gunn. "He didn't have much education. He cut rail ties and then he worked as a janitor for the county courthouse here."

In the years after World War II, when Gunn operated several Cripple Creek mines, Coplen showed up looking for work. "I didn't have anything," says Gunn. "Poor old

George."

George Coplen died in the 1960s. He is buried at Mount Pisgah Cemetery in Cripple Creek. But neither he nor Dempsey is neglected by the community. On the second floor of the Cripple Creek Museum, a first-rate showplace filled with a century's worth of lore and artifacts, stands a glass display case. Behind a locked door is a pair of light brown boxing gloves. The gloves, worn smooth as a cavalry saddle, are the ones Dempsey used the night he thought the building had blown up under his feet.

Whenever Francis Gunn walks by that display case he thinks about Jack Dempsey—a man with a fighting heart. A man with a big heart. "When George Coplen was down on his luck," says Gunn, "he used to hit up Dempsey for money. This was long after both men had quit the ring. Far as I know Dempsey never turned down poor old George."

CHAPTER VII

Vagabond

"Surviving. That's what being a hobo was all about."

As a boy in Manassa, Jack Dempsey used to lie awake at night—he slept in the family cabin's attic loft—and listen for the far off sound of train whistles. Ever since, railroads represented something adventurous and romantic to Dempsey. Railroads signified opportunity. And beginning with the unhappy experience in Leadville, when a conductor threatened to throw him off a train, railroads played a large role in Dempsey's Colorado days.

The steam railroad most often used by Dempsey was the Denver and Rio Grande. In Colorado seventy-five years ago, the D&RG ran almost everywhere Dempsey worked: from copper mining encampments to cattle ranches. The D&RG huffed and puffed across the state, roughly following the line that U.S. 50 now travels. The railroad went into southern Colorado, spreading itself from border to border, from Springfield to Cortez, like a giant spiderweb of narrow-gauge and standard track.

The rail line began in 1871 as the brainchild of William Jackson Palmer, a plucky little Philadelphian. Originally, Palmer planned to connect Denver with Mexico City. He didn't get that far, but he went a good many miles. And Dempsey traveled much of the way with his line.

Dempsey got to know the railroad from the ground up. Since he seldom had much money in his youth, Dempsey learned from his brother Bern and others how to climb aboard a train's brake rods and ride like a hobo. Often Dempsey traveled hundreds of miles this way just to say hello to his mother. Dempsey didn't particularly relish the vagabond lifestyle. But he needed to do it to live.

In later years, Dempsey on occasion tried to play down the fact that from 1911-1916 he had been a hobo. He was afraid people would confuse hobo with bum. A hobo is a migratory worker. A tramp is a migratory nonworker. A bum is a non-migratory nonworker. "I was never a bum," Dempsey argued. "Or even a tramp."

When there were booms in Colorado—gold, silver, copper, coal—Dempsey rode for miles to try to cash in on the job market. He'd travel for hours on a brake beam to pick apples all day for a wage that today wouldn't buy breakfast. Dempsey was able to do this and not weaken and become a bum because, in the back of his mind, he kept hoping that somehow, someday, he'd become champion. Simply, the dream kept him going.

The closest Dempsey came to being a bum were those times when he did what many hoboes did who were down on their luck. Flat broke in some strange Colorado town, he would search for the best-looking house, go to the back door, and knock.

"M'am," Dempsey would say to the woman of the house. "Might you have some chores a fella could do in exchange for a meal or a few cents?"

Often the woman had a pile of logs that needed splitting or a garage that had to be cleaned or a garden to be tilled. Dempsey accommodated. Unlike the poor peddler who came to his mother's house in Manassa with the John L. Sullivan book, Dempsey did not beg. He worked whenever he could. "I never turned down a job anybody offered me. No matter what the pay."

And he never stole. "I'd rather go hungry than steal."

Hoboing took root in this country in the late 1880s and flourished through the Great Depression. Novelist John Steinbeck referred to hoboes as "the last free men." Today, few hobo "jungles" or camps, remain. The future of the hobo is, in fact, endangered.

But in Jack Dempsey's early days, hoboes were as common as crows. That more railroads operated then explains their abundance. By the end of the nineteenth century, railroads reached every county in the United States. Almost 200,000 miles of track crisscrossed America.

When Dempsey returned to Colorado in 1911 after living in Utah for two years, he caught his first alfresco train ride. He traveled from Provo, Utah, to Grand Junction, Colorado, by lying on two-inch-wide steel rods beneath a Pullman. At Grand Junction he hopped a freight train, balancing himself on one car's brake beams. His ride wasn't particularly successful. He wound up not in Montrose but in Palisade, Colorado, where he found work in a peach orchard. Eventually Dempsey quit the fruit-gathering job—it paid only two dollars a day—when his boss told him to stop singing while he picked.

Living in a quintessential railroad town like Montrose gave Dempsey a thorough knowledge of riding trains for free. He learned to "read" a freight train. That meant not only discovering where a train was headed, but finding the best place on it to ride. Traveling inside a boxcar meant Dempsey had to pay off the "bulls," or policemen, who threw hoboes off trains. So he occasionally rode in a gondola, an open-topped boxcar, or even on the roof, or "deck," of a passenger car. A much tougher ride was on the "death woods," the spot above the coupling on boxcars. Other bad seats were the cowcatcher in front of the engine and the pile of ashes in the coal car. A "reefer," or refrigerator car, was a possibility. But a hobo had to be careful when dealing with a reefer. If a bull decided to lock a reefer door, the hobo inside froze to death.

The rods—strips attached to a Pullman's belly—were Dempsey's best bet. But even they were no bargain. A vagabond could easily fall off of them.

Dempsey found other dangers in riding the rods. "Yeggs" (itinerant criminals) plagued hobo camps. Tuberculosis, rheumatism, and homosexual rape also were prevalent. Perhaps the biggest threat was from accidents. The Interstate Commerce Commission reported that nearly 25,000 railroad trespassers were killed between 1910 and 1915. Many towns during that period had their own hobo graveyards.

Dempsey often emerged from train rides grime-covered and wearing a thick growth of beard. Sometimes he carried a "bindle," or rolled up knapsack on a pole. Other times he carried nothing. Whenever he reached a destination or a job, he "boiled up," or washed, his clothes and body to kill the vermin of the rails.

Wherever he went Dempsey sang this railroad ditty

known by all hoboes:

> *You will eat, bye and bye,*
> *In that glorious land in the sky;*
> *Work and pray, live on hay*
> *You'll get pie in the sky when you die.*

During Dempsey's Colorado days he ran into many celebrated hoboes, such as Hairbreadth Harry, Scoopshovel Scotty and Boxcar Barney. Dempsey, of course, had his own nickname: Kid Blackie.

Hoboing taught Kid Blackie a way to size up the country's economy: long cigarette butts on the ground meant prosperity; short ones signaled hard times ahead. Hoboing also taught him which towns had jobs and which did not. And it taught him which communities to stay away from and which would be generous. The more charitable towns always seemed to be the ones where the circus was stopped.

"There was a strong bond of brotherhood among hoboes," Dempsey said. "And I felt it right away. Hoboes didn't try to pry into your business or affairs. They helped each other."

Dempsey had the same good feeling for railroads. His father and brothers had worked for railroads. He got to know many station agents and telegraph operators throughout Colorado and culled information from them. For instance, he learned that mail trains, zipping along at seventy miles per hour, offered fast rides across the state, but trains rushing perishable goods to market went even faster. Dempsey came to respect railroads. He never forgot to tie his hands and feet to the rods with strong cloth, or chains even, to avoid slipping off and dying if he fell asleep. In later years Dempsey compared his teenage travels with today's hitchhiking: an enterprising but sometimes hazardous means of getting from one place to another without spending money.

Sometimes that means of transportation took strange turns. In 1916, Dempsey briefly departed Colorado to test the boxing waters in New York City. Because he had saved a few dollars, Dempsey rode the cushions all the way. When he left New York after a few months, however, he was

After he won the heavyweight title in 1919, Dempsey showed a flair for clothing.

destitute. Thus Dempsey returned to Colorado via the rods.

After stopping for a while in Pueblo, Colorado, Dempsey took off with a neophyte male hobo named "Liz" Fisher. It was a bitter cold night when they left Pueblo. Fisher's teeth chattered furiously as the pair clutched the brake rods. When they arrived at the edge of a western Colorado town the next morning, Dempsey took Fisher to a hobo jungle and dropped him off while he went to look for something to eat.

A beautiful young woman opened the first door Dempsey knocked on. Dempsey went into his speech about doing chores.

"I don't have any work," the woman interrupted, "but I'll get you something else."

In a few minutes the woman returned with a paper sack filled with cheeses, rolls, bread, fruit, turkey and ham.

Stunned, Dempsey tipped his cap and raced back to the jungle. There, Liz Fisher waited, still shivering.

"Sorry, pal," Dempsey kiddingly told his friend. "I didn't have any luck." Dempsey loved practical jokes. He liked giving people hotfoots or pulling chairs out from under them. But Liz Fisher didn't go for this joke at all. Dempsey's news made him cry.

"Hey, pal," Dempsey said, surprised. "Look." From his jacket Dempsey pulled out the paper bag. Both men went at the food ravenously.

The two were finishing the last bite when three policemen entered the jungle. "We're taking you in," the cops told Dempsey, Fisher and a couple of other hoboes. This was no practical joke.

The town was Salida, Colorado. With a big bowling tournament coming up, the local alley needed help. The alley's owner had coerced the police to round up men— hoboes, even—to set pins.

That Salida bowling alley stood on First Street. The late Ted Judge, a long-time Salidan, remembered the day the police pulled Dempsey into town. "Other than his clothes and dirt, you'd never know he'd been a hobo. He was a pretty good bowler and had set pins before."

Judge recalled the hobo in the lane next to Dempsey. Attempting to send a ball back to a bowler, the hobo dropped the ball on Dempsey's hand. Dempsey cried in pain as the hand swelled. The ball had mashed two fingers.

"It's a wonder," said Judge, "that he didn't ruin his boxing career right there."

Hoboing helped Dempsey become a better boxer. It made him more alert in times of danger, for instance, and showed him that nothing in life or in a boxing ring came easily.

More than anything else, perhaps, hoboing across Colorado as "Kid Blackie" forced Dempsey to depend on himself. In a prizefight against a tougher or bigger opponent, there would be nobody to call upon for help.

After Dempsey became internationally known, his vagabond days didn't seem, he felt, to fit with his new image. Meanwhile, Jack Kearns, Dempsey's manager during the 1920s and a master of ballyhoo, played up the hoboing. Dempsey's dark complexion, Kearns explained, was the result of flying cinders becoming embedded under his skin.

After Dempsey beat Willard in 1919, for the heavyweight championship, and the press began interviewing him with great regularity, Dempsey announced that he had never stolen rides on trains. After he defended his title against Georges Carpentier, in 1921, Dempsey told Damon Runyon, the famous New York sportswriter, "Let's forget this hobo business now. We want to be gentlemen after this."

But Runyon, a friend of Dempsey's since 1916, knew better. "Anyone who has traveled the country with Dempsey," Runyon wrote, "and seen the weird characters that bob up to him in every town, mumbling of the old days of eating out of tin cans or sharing a pot of mulligan stew, knows Jack couldn't have met them in drawing rooms."

Surely Dempsey's most desperate experience as a vagabond occurred in 1913. At the Grand Junction rail yard he caught a train on the run for Delta. As Dempsey pulled himself up on a freight car by grabbing a ladder, a railroad bull yelled for him to get off. Dempsey hung on, however; the train by now was going too fast for him to jump off. Angered at Dempsey's refusal to let go, the bull, who was riding the train, clambered over to where Dempsey was and began hitting him with a billy club.

"I'll teach you to get offa here!" the policeman screamed as he bashed at Dempsey's head.

Finally, his scalp split open like a grapefruit, Dempsey blacked out and fell off the train. He rolled and tumbled in the rocks and rubble. After he regained consciousness, Dempsey walked, with blood dripping from his head, the forty miles to Delta.

"Surviving," said Dempsey of the incident. "That's what being a hobo was all about."

CHAPTER VIII

Victor

"Most people here felt Jack was kind of an arrogant or spoiled kid. At least back then."

Cripple Creek may have been the social and financial center of Colorado's gold mining region, but Victor, its neighbor to the south, was where the miners lived and where most of the gold came from.

Because it sits in Cripple Creek's shadow, Victor suffers an identification problem. Its name is plain, no one has written a song about the town and tourists don't flock there. Yet if Cripple Creek was "the World's Greatest Gold Camp," Victor was "the City of Mines." At one time Victor had fifty mines and 26,000 patented mining claims.

Victor grew nearly as fast as Cripple. By 1908 Victor had 17,000 people. Today it has about 500 in the summer and perhaps one-third that during the winter.

As in Cripple, some gold still lies buried beneath the hills surrounding Victor. But currently it would take, as the expression goes, seven dollars to pull one dollar's worth of ore from the ground.

Jack Dempsey helped to pull gold out of Victor during his vagabonding days of 1913 and 1914. Dempsey came to the town because the mines were hiring and because Victor had a boxing tradition similar to Cripple Creek's. Lum Myberg, also known as "The Golden Boy," was a Victor welterweight in the early days of this century. Myberg fought two important bouts with Eddie Eagan of Longmont, Colorado, who later won an Olympic gold medal in boxing. In the first bout, in Denver, Myberg beat Eagan. In the rematch, held in Victor, Eagan knocked out Myberg in the sixth round.

Victor produced during the 1920s a flyweight named Eddie West who carved a fair reputation fighting on the West Coast.

The name Morgan Williams, however, stands out in

Victor boxing annals—perhaps even more so than Jack Dempsey. Morg Williams made a name for himself as a professional fighter and as a manger. Williams, who started fighting before 1900, twice fought Fireman Jim Flynn, a boxer who would later give Dempsey trouble. In 1904, Flynn decisioned Williams in Pueblo in twenty rounds. Rematches had a way of being postponed in those days. Eleven years after their first bout, Williams and Flynn tangled again, this time in Victor. In that fight Flynn knocked out the Victor resident in fourteen rounds.

If Morg Williams had trouble with Flynn, he had no problems with George Coplen, Dempsey's Cripple Creek foe. Williams floored Coplen in two rounds at the old Victor Opera House.

When Morg Williams wasn't fighting, he was teaching boxing to Victor's young men in a room above city hall. One of Williams' pupils was Lowell Thomas. "All the boys of that particular age wanted to be prizefighters," Thomas wrote in his autobiography. Born in Ohio, Lowell Thomas was raised in Victor. His father had gone West to become Victor's doctor. Thomas graduated from Victor High School in 1910 and worked for two newspapers in town before leaving Colorado and eventually gaining worldwide fame as a radio commentator.

Morg Williams also taught Jack Dempsey. Williams helped get Dempsey some fights in town: two at the Gold Coin Club, another at the Victor Opera House, plus some sessions at the Victor Union and Armory halls.

No shortage of boxing opponents existed in the City of Mines. Victor's steeply sloped streets bustled with hoisters, timbermen, tram men and other mine laborers who liked to raise their fists. Filling out a fight audience were "upper tens," mine owners and superintendents in high starched collars, who liked to place big bets.

When Dempsey first arrived in Victor he was still bellying up to bars as "Kid Blackie" and offering to fight anyone in the joint. However, his voice by now had matured. His nose had been broken a few times and small dents creased his face. He looked and sounded tough, but so did just about everybody in a mining camp saloon.

When he wasn't working at the Portland, one of the biggest mines in Victor, or training with Morg Williams, Dempsey headed for one of the many water holes—the Monarch or the Diamond, for instance—in Victor's tenderloin section. Once in a while he dropped in at Dingman's gambling emporium. He didn't drink and never had enough money to gamble; anything extra went home to his mother in Utah. Dempsey just liked to shoot the breeze with fellow miners.

Those were good times. Years later Dempsey still remembered a song he sang often in Victor with a bunch of men whose scratchy-flat voices were as off-key as his own. The ditty went like this:

> *If I was a millionaire and had a lot of coin,*
> *I would plant a row of coke plantations and grow*
> *Heroyn,*
> *I would have Camel cigarettes growin' on my*
> *trees,*
> *I'd build a castle of morphine and live there at*
> *my ease.*
> *I would have forty thousand hop layouts, each one*
> *inlaid with pearls.*
> *I'd invite each old time fighter to bring along his*
> *girl.*
> *And everyone who had a habit,*
> *I'd have them leaping like a rabbit,*
> *Down at the fighters' jublilee!*
>
> *Down at the fighters' jubilee!*
> *Down on the Isle of H.M. and C.*
>
> *H. stands for heroyn, M. stands for morph,*
> *C. for cokoloro—to blow your head off.*
> *Autos and airships and big sirloin steaks,*
> *Each old time fighter would own his own lake.*
>
> *We'll build castles in the air,*
> *And all feel like millionaires,*
> *Down at the fighters' jubilee!*

Done in unison, the song amused Dempsey. Later, however, it made him sad. Dempsey's brother Johnny died from using hard drugs.

———————

*One critic blamed Dempsey's early writing efforts
on his failure to remove boxing gloves while typing.*

Dempsey had his photograph taken in Victor for probably
the first time in his life. Wearing boxing trunks, he posed
barefisted, his hands filthy from mining. The expression on
his young face was anxious yet slightly dazed.

William Lehr took the photograph. Lehr captured on film
much of early-day Victor as well as the boxers under the
tutelage of Morgan Williams. Lehr worked for the Victor
Fire Department when he wasn't taking pictures. He is
remembered as a volunteer fireman who once wrote proudly
in the firehouse logbook of a blaze that destroyed a home:
"Saved the lot and well."

Thirty years after his Victor sojourn Dempsey visited
Denver to attend a banquet. As he was getting dressed on
the gala evening, Dempsey heard a knock at the door of his
room in the Brown Palace Hotel. When he opened the door,

a wizened little man, hat in hand, stood waiting.

"Are you Kid Blackie?" the visitor asked.

Dempsey laughed at the name from the faraway past. "Sure," he said. "I guess. Who are you?"

"I'm W.H. Lehr and you owe me a buck and a quarter. You never paid for those photos I took of you."

Because he liked to kid around, Dempsey wondered if this might be a joke. Then he realized the little man was serious. "Well," Dempsey said, "the pictures were no good."

"Oh, yes they were," Lehr said. With that he reached into his coat pocket and pulled out a wrinkled but still clear shot of a gangling Dempsey in a boxing stance.

Suddenly Dempsey remembered how he had come to Victor in 1914 by riding the rods, and how he had seen an advertisement in Lehr's shop window: "Photographs, $1.25." Dead broke, Dempsey had persuaded Lehr to take his picture. He promised to repay the photographer the first chance he got. In a rush to leave town for a fight he had forgotten. But W.H. Lehr hadn't.

One of Lehr's photographs of Dempsey now hangs over the bar of the Gold Coin Saloon, Victor's principal restaurant. The stepchild of the Gold Coin Club, the saloon serves one of the best cheeseburgers in Colorado. Lehr's photo peers out from a row of beer steins. Dempsey autographed the picture in 1928. For several years, Lillian Clark, who ran the Gold Coin, answered questions about the photo. "Yes," she told visitors, "Jack Dempsey fought here. No, I wasn't around back then."

In 1914, the year Dempsey spent the most time in Victor, gold production slipped. Still, that year the mines produced about thirteen million dollars' worth of ore. Dempsey always enjoyed any kind of mining, perhaps because he missed out on the bad parts of the job. He never suffered an accident or the consequences of an employment strike. Dempsey was too young to experience the bloody 1904 Cripple Creek labor wars that left thirty-three dead. When a walkout hit the coal mines of Trinidad, Colorado, in 1914, and five miners and one soldier were killed in the turmoil, Dempsey was elsewhere.

Dempsey started out as a mucker in Victor's mines. A mucker was the last man in a hole. He trailed the machine men, or miners, who came first. The timbermen, the fellows who braced the hole, were next. Then the muckers. The muckers' job was to load loose ore into cars and then push those cars to the shaft where the ore was then hoisted to the surface.

Dempsey worked intermittently for six months as a mucker. Then he became an assistant foreman. Next, he put in a spell as a hoistman. Eventually he became a full-fledged miner.

A miner cut holes into the rock wall at the end of a drift or passageway with drills or jackhammers. Single-jackers were followed by double-jackers—two men working together. One would hit the wall while the other held the drill. Power drills that used compressed air came later.

Safety always was a factor in gold mining. Dempsey's biggest worries concerned dynamite and falling rock. There existed the temptation to be impatient after a dynamite charge was set into one of the eight holes on an underground rock face. Not waiting long enough for that charge to go off could blow a miner to bits.

And there always was the chance that the timbermen did not do their job well enough. No miner liked to look up and see a ceiling of ore and dirt falling like black rain.

Still, Dempsey savored gold mining. "I always felt wonderful deep in a mine." Certainly mining did good things for his body. Long hours wielding a heavy sledge gave him Popeye forearms. Alternating a drill between his left and right hands built up Dempsey's shoulders and made him nearly ambidextrous, a distinct advantage for any boxer.

"Jack Dempsey lived right here," says a lean and rangy man with thinning white hair. He is standing beside a multi-level house on a hill at the west end of Victor.

The man is Joe Vanderwalker. He was born in Victor more than eighty years ago. Dr. Harry George Thomas, Lowell's father, signed his birth certificate.

Now retired after working fifty years for the Southern Colorado Power Company, mostly in the Rocky Ford and Ordway, Colorado, areas, Vanderwalker does odd jobs around Victor. In the summertime he helps out at the Victor School of Photography, a nationally recognized workshop housed in the town's old high school.

Joe Vanderwalker lives with a German shepherd named Chip in the multi-level house, a comfortable wooden structure attached to a small cabin. Years ago Jack Dempsey lived in the cabin periodically while he worked at the Portland Mine. "I don't know how he paid for the place," says Vanderwalker, stroking Chip. "As a mucker he couldn't have been making over three dollars a day."

Grabbing a Bavarian-style wool hat, Vanderwalker begins a guided tour of Victor as it pertained to Jack Dempsey. As he walks down the town's main street, Vanderwalker explains that his father came to Victor in 1891 from Oskaloosa, Iowa, where he had mined coal. But George Vanderwalker could not get a job in Victor. "He was a labor sympathizer," reveals his son. "No one would hire him."

The family was forced to move ten miles outside of town to Phantom Canyon. George Vanderwalker took what jobs he could—carpenter, roustabout. For a couple of years the Vanderwalkers lived in New Mexico while George hunted mining jobs in Arizona. Still considered a threat to management, Vanderwalker remained unemployed. He eventually took his family back to Victor. Finally, in 1927, a mine hired George. "By then," says Joe Vanderwalker, his face clouded with sadness and anger, "the mines here had started to go downhill."

At the Victor City Hall, a stately red brick building, Vanderwalker leads the way up a flight of stairs. "This is where all the boxers used to train with Morg Williams," Vanderwalker says, stopping at a white-walled back room. Pausing at a spot where a large punching bag once swung from the ceiling, Vanderwalker continues, "You know, I'm not the biggest Jack Dempsey fan in the world. Sure, I liked him when I was a kid here. But then I found out what he did to Morg Williams. The two of them went out to the West Coast together, Morg serving as Dempsey's manager. When Jack started to do well in California, he left old Morg high and dry. Just dumped him. Morg came back to Victor flat broke."

Leaving city hall, Vanderwalker moves through the heart

of Victor. He stops at an intersection. Many of Victor's handsome buildings still stand. A few of the old structures cater to tourists: a rock shop here, an antiques store there. Other buildings are boarded up. Victor is not nearly as commercial as Cripple Creek. Major fires struck both towns around the turn of the century. The blazes leveled most of each community's wooden buildings. When Victor rebuilt, the townspeople used brick.

Up a steep side street Vanderwalker halts in front of a vacant four-story building. "This was Pat Sullivan's saloon," he says. "One time Dempsey went in here and picked up a beer that didn't belong to him. It belonged to Jim Sullivan, Pat's son. Well, Jim got mad and took Dempsey outside and fought him, right in this gutter. Guess who won? Jim Sullivan. That's the truth."

Continuing a few more blocks, Vanderwalker pauses at a spot now home to a small tourist depot. "Right here stood the Victor Opera House. Used to be owned by a man named Lemaster. It was brick, but it burned too. The Opera House was a nice place inside. Had a balcony and two stairways on either side. It was built about 1900 and was pretty fancy. There were screens on the back end that were raised and lowered by rope blocks. It had four box seats. It would be a showplace now. Too bad."

Joe Vanderwalker never saw Dempsey fight in the Opera House, but he did see Dempsey's trainer and manager, Morg Williams battle Fireman Jim Flynn there.

"Flynn said, 'Hit me.' When poor Morg did he broke both his hands."

As he backtracks up Main Street, Vanderwalker says that the only time he paid any attention to Dempsey after the boxer left Victor was when a photograph appeared in a Colorado Springs newspaper. Dempsey and a woman were riding a burro at the Garden of the Gods.

"I think most people here felt he was kind of an arrogant or spoiled kid. At least back then. Dempsey may not have been like that later, but I do know that son of a gun never came back to Victor. Lowell Thomas used to come back to Victor year after year. But not Jack Dempsey."

Joe Vanderwalker on the second floor of the Victor City Hall, where Kid Blackie trained.

CHAPTER IX

Durango

"He was hungry back then. You could see it in his eyes."

There may be little recollection of the early Jack Dempsey in Telluride, but fifty miles across the San Juan Mountains, in Durango, Colorado, the boxer in his youth is on public display.

Gracing the exterior north wall of the El Rancho Lounge, on the corner of Tenth and Main streets in downtown Durango, is a twenty-by-thirty-foot mural. The painting, completed in September, 1980, depicts a Dempsey bout held in Durango on October 7, 1915.

After fighting for almost a year in California and Nevada, with only periodic trips back to Colorado, Dempsey returned to his home state in late 1915 to once again join forces with Andy Malloy. Following a brief stint in Montrose, the pair was summoned to Durango by Buck Weaver, a barber/sports promoter originally from Pueblo.

That year and the next were not good ones for Dempsey as a boxer. More and more he found it difficult to obtain fights. The situation depressed him. He still was unknown and there would be no gain for anyone in beating Kid Blackie. And yet, as Dempsey's reputation widened, better fighters began to duck him. Managers were not much help to him, either. If one found him a fight, it usually was with a canvas-back whom Dempsey could drop in minutes.

The sad part was that Dempsey improved significantly during 1915. He still looked a bit strange with his close-cropped hair, scarecrow-thin legs and an American flag that he often strung between the belt loops of his pants. However, in the ring Kid Blackie was no bumpkin. Andy and Pat Malloy and all the stiffs Dempsey had met in his mining camp days had taught him a great deal. By 1915 he had learned to get his entire weight behind a punch, to pivot, to hit straight from the shoulder, and to follow through on a punch.

The Durango fight seemed like a good chance for Dempsey to sharpen his skills. As a challenge, however, it would offer nothing stringent. Dempsey would be pitted against his old friend Andy Malloy.

The fight took place at the Gem Theater on a Thursday evening. Promotions had gotten better since the Fred Wood days: reserved seats went on sale at Richey's, a business-supply store, for two dollars. General admission tickets sold for one dollar.

"A lot of people in Durango used to say they went to that fight," says Dr. Duane Smith, a history professor at Durango's Fort Lewis College. "But I think it's like the people who say they saw Babe Ruth pointing where he wanted to hit a home run. A lot of people *thought* they saw it."

One person who did witness the fight is Louis Smith. Born in 1891, Smith stands erect and clear-eyed. His voice is strong and his face remarkably unlined. Smith has lived a good part of his life in Durango on a plot of land about one-half mile from the Gem Theater. Several times a week Smith walks the half mile downtown, past where the Gem stood and by the mural, in a forceful and determined stride.

Louis Smith's father came to Durango in 1882 to work for the Denver and Rio Grande Railroad. The senior Smith built a home on Third Street and farmed when he wasn't on duty as a railroad engineer.

As a young man, Louis helped out on the family farm. In his free time he played kick-the-can under the arc lights that illuminated Durango at night. Or he shadowboxed with friends. Smith quit school in the seventh grade. "I got discouraged," he says while pausing from the tiny but flourishing garden he tends in front of his house. "I never did learn a trade. It's been a hard life all the way through."

When Jack Dempsey came to town, Smith was working as a laborer on Durango's streets—digging out rocks, putting in water lines, building board sidewalks. "That's how I caught news of the fight—from the fellows who worked with me."

Though he'd never officially fought in the town, Dempsey had been to Durango before. He had traveled over snowy Red Mountain Pass from Ouray and had briefly worked in the City Coal Mine and in the Porter Mine at Wildcat

Canyon. Dempsey liked coal mining nearly as much as hard-rock mining. He appreciated the close-knit ties among coal miners and the concern they had for safety. Most coal miners, Dempsey found, checked to make sure that short squibs of powder were detonated and that shafts were shored up after a blast before work continued. Dempsey didn't even mind the coal dust that collected in his fingernails, hair, nose and ears. "I'm the only man I ever knew who actually enjoys going to a mine to fight chunks of coal off a wall."

When Dempsey came to Durango in 1915 he traded coal dust for milk. "He moved in with the Conroy family," says Louis Smith, putting on a straw hat to shield his naked scalp from the sun. "Mike Conroy had a dairy in Animas City, on the outskirts of town. The place is still there but not working. The Conroys got stuck on Dempsey. They thought he was the greatest guy in the world. Jack delivered milk for Mike. I used to see Jack on the milk wagon in the morning. He was a dark kid, skinny but athletic looking. He seemed like a fellow who could run and jump on a boxcar, which he did."

Between jobs as a miner, hod carrier, lumberjack and laborer, Dempsey tried to stay in condition. When he couldn't find a gym to work out in, he did roadwork, knocking off five or six miles at a time. But a job such as coal mining proved a good substitute. It added muscle to his lower back and built up his lung power.

The Durango fight took place, according to Smith, "because things were dull around here." In truth, the week of the fight was anything but dull. The annual Colorado-New Mexico Fair, the biggest event in the Four Corners area, had just opened. (During the 1913 fair, Durango saw its first airplane.) In addition, the sports pages that week were filled, not with stories about boxing, but with articles on baseball. The World Series began that week. The Boston Red Sox faced the Philadelphia Phillies. Thus, the Dempsey-Malloy bout received scant attention from the press. The Durango newspapers *did* note that the doors at the Gem would open at 10:00 p.m. on fight night.

Though it did not rival its neighbor Telluride in wide-open vice, Durango in Jack Dempsey's youth was a lively town—a bit conservative, perhaps, because of its position as the county seat of La Plata County. Still, the strip along Main Street, where the Gem Theater stood, was known as the "Saloon Block." The Saloon Block featured a squadron of sporting houses, a famous madam named Bessie Rivers, an opium den or two and a few taverns. All in all a modest honky-tonk.

Conservatism didn't run everywhere in Durango, however. Dave Day, the crusading editor of the local newspaper,

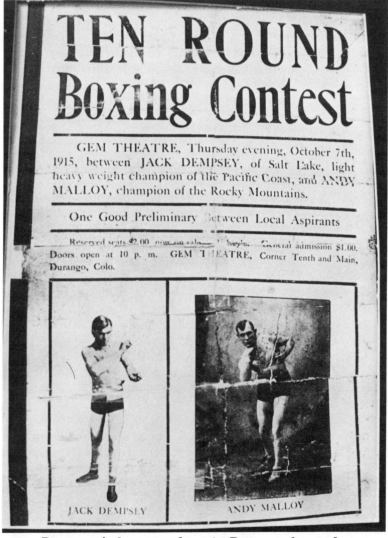

Dempsey's long-ago bout in Durango has today become a poster prized by collectors.

wrote in 1914: "Sunday baseball is preferable to the average Sunday sermon."

"I wasn't much for going to the Saloon Block," admits Louis Smith. However, Smith's friend, John Zumbush, a bricklayer and town character, was. Smith can remember the afternoon that Zumbush sat on a railing in front of the Central Hotel, on the Saloon Block. From an upstairs window, a sporting lady threw a basin of water on Zumbush. "He got soaked," says Smith, chuckling at the memory. "And everybody else got a good laugh. This was right around the time of the Dempsey fight."

Approximately two hundred people crowded down the Gem Theater's sloping aisles on that October evening in 1915. The ring stood on the stage, down low, like an arena. Durango sheriff Arthur Fassbinder announced prior to the fight that if either Dempsey or Malloy were knocked out, he would arrest both participants. This was, after all, an era when public fighting was not universally accepted. Therefore, the fight had to be billed as an "exhibition."

The exhibition lasted ten rounds. Though no winner was acknowledged, years later Dempsey recalled giving Malloy some "stiff wallops." The Durango *Herald Evening Democrat* reported that "the audience declared Dempsey the better man."

"He *was* better," says Smith, who was there. Oddly, some people in Durango always figured that Malloy, who was far past his prime at this point, would become a nationally recognized boxer, not Dempsey. Malloy, however, must have realized that as a fighter he would never make it beyond Colorado. That thought caused him to continue to give Dempsey free advice.

"If you fight a man once," Malloy told Dempsey in Durango just prior to their bout, "make mental notes for future fights with the same man."

Not surprisingly, each time Dempsey fought Andy Malloy he picked up something new and saved it. Weaving, for example. By watching Malloy, Dempsey learned to duck his head from side to side. The move enabled him to throw a great number of hard blows in a short time. Consequently, bobbing from side to side made Dempsey harder to hit, and at the same time, it gave him a two-fisted attack that alternated fast and powerful right- and left-handed blows.

Later in his career, whenever Dempsey had a rematch with another boxer, and he had several, he almost always did much better the second time around.

Though Malloy was right-handed, he taught Dempsey in 1915 how to employ a shift against southpaws. "Miss the guy with your right on purpose." Malloy said. "Then while your opponent is thinking about that, sneak in your left to the jaw."

———————

Not long after Dempsey's Durango fight, Louis Smith moved to the West Coast. He worked for a time on ranches in California and Oregon. "I had to take whatever I could get." When Gene Tunney beat Dempsey for the title in 1926, Smith was working in Riverside, California. "I was washing off some Hereford cattle that were going to be shown at a county fair. Sure I felt sad when I heard the news. I kind of admired Dempsey. To me he was more or less local."

Smith returned to Durango in the 1930s and took a series of menial jobs. He was married for thirty-nine years but had no children. "My wife and I were kind of disappointed in our youth. We didn't want that for our offspring." In 1939, Smith and his wife, Leona, moved into a second-floor apartment behind the home where he was born. A widower, Smith lives where he and his wife did, up a flight of wooden stairs in a tidy four-room flat. Down below is his thriving flower garden. "That's what occupies most of my time now. The flowers."

Louis and Leona Smith liked to attend the Gem Theater, not to see boxing, but wrestling, or "rassling," as Smith calls it. Fifty years ago a Durango promoter named Nick Collins brought "rassling" to the Gem when movies weren't being shown. One of the last films Smith saw at the Gem—for a dime, he thinks—was "that Civil War thing" (*Gone With the Wind*).

Part of the Gem became an ice cream parlor. Then a bookstore. Now it is The Cut Loose. "I'm not sure what Jack Dempsey would have thought of that," says Smith. "The Cut Loose. That's a ladies' haircut place."

———————

Dempsey was a vague memory in Durango until artist Tom McMurray convinced the Chamber of Commerce that a mural highlighting the boxer would be a nice addition to the downtown. "It's been good for business, I hear," says Smith, who has left his garden this day to walk to the mural. When he reaches the painting, Smith stops, removes his straw hat and wipes his head with a handkerchief. "I think it's a fine piece of work. Even though it ain't quite accurate."

The painting is located just south of the old Gem Theater and a few blocks north of the Durango train depot, the starting point of the celebrated Durango-Silverton line. Jack Dempsey once rode that train, but not as a paying sightseer. More people ride the train in a year now than rode it in a decade during Dempsey's time.

McMurray's mural, done in rich, earthy browns and blacks, captures through muted colors a bygone era. What Louis Smith questions is the artist's research. A placard on the mural indicates the fight took place in the Central Hotel, which occupies the upstairs of the El Rancho Lounge. For many years Durango citizens believed that the fight *did* go on at the Central, mainly because the bar and hotel once were the site of boxing matches. Louis Smith says no; the fight took place at the Gem. Smith remembers the El Rancho when it was the Oxford Bar. In the basement of the Oxford stood a makeshift ring and wooden benches for spectators. "The rest of the time they held gambling down there."

The Oxford—later it became the American Bar and even later served as the town's post office—was a hangout for laborers and sawmill workers. The Central Hotel also catered to a blue-collar crowd. Both establishments have since been remodeled. Now most of their customers are tourists.

McMurray's mural, painted directly on the red brick wall of the El Rancho, is clearly visible to anyone headed toward the train depot. When Louis Smith walks by the mural, he frequently smiles. The two antagonists in the painting are wearing long pants. Smith knows that while boxers years ago dressed like that, they did not fight in that garb in Durango in 1915. A photograph of Dempsey and Malloy, taken by R.W. Rowland, a prolific turn-of-the-century Durango photographer, shows both boxers in trunks.

On the floor of McMurray's ring is an open bottle of whiskey. "I don't know what that's doing there," says

Smith, resting his arm against a parking meter in front of the mural. "For effect, I suppose." Towels are draped over chairs in the painting. "It wasn't that hot that night," recollects Smith. "Remember, this was October."

Though knockouts were not allowed, Dempsey in the painting is standing over Malloy, who is sprawled on the floor and is obviously in a stupor. "That's about what happened," says Smith. "Malloy got whipped. You can see Malloy wasn't in great shape. Look at the way his stomach hangs out like a tub of guts."

The referee in the mural is a stout gent sporting a walrus mustache, tie and vest. He holds a pocket watch in one hand. "That's Arthur Fassbinder, the sheriff," Smith points out. "He was honest and fair. A good man."

Dempsey was a good man, too, according to Smith. Dempsey returned to Durango in the 1930s, says Smith, to give his sister Stella a proper burial. Stella Dempsey had been working as a waitress in town. When she died she was laid to rest in a pauper's graveyard. Dempsey had her body moved to Durango's Greenmount Cemetery.

Dempsey once recalled that he received thirty dollars for the Durango fight. "I'm not sure he got *that* much," says Smith. "He was hungry back then. You could see it in his eyes. Whatever Dempsey got paid, he probably spent on food the next day."

Shortly after the Durango exhibition, Andy Malloy, still trying to act as Dempsey's manager, got his fighter a bout in Olathe, Colorado, a potato-producing hamlet about 120 miles north of Durango.

Dempsey's opponent was the local Olathe strong man, a boxer/wrestler named simply "Big Ed." Since Big Ed was considered a better wrestler than boxer, Malloy made the match a winner-take-all deal. Malloy figured Dempsey would outbox Big Ed in a matter of seconds.

Malloy and Dempsey checked into a five-dollar-a-week room at an Olathe boardinghouse. By now Dempsey was rested from Durango and was raring to go. "The thing I looked forward to most," he said, "was my next fight. I was

Louis Smith and the Durango mural: "I think it's a fine piece of work. Even though it ain't quite accurate."

never happy till I knew it was scheduled."

The Olathe fight was not to be, however. Just before the start of the contest, held in the town's livery stable, the Olathe marshal, burly Paris Gaines, stepped into the stable wearing a frown on his face. "We don't permit boxing in this town," Gaines told Dempsey and his manager.

"Huh?" said the astonished Dempsey.

"I'll tell you what I'll do though," said the marshal. "You can wrestle Ed if you like."

"But I'm a boxer, not a wrestler," Dempsey protested. He turned to Malloy. "Andy, I'll get killed wrestling. Let's get out of here."

Paris Gaines, however, had other ideas. "Son," said the marshal, placing a hand on Dempsey's shoulder. "Your landlady told me you ain't paid your five dollars' rent yet. If you don't cough up, I'm gonna have to toss the both of you in jail."

Again, Dempsey looked at Malloy. Each knew what the other was thinking. Flat broke, they were depending on the outcome of the fight to pay for the room. Therefore, Dempsey *had* to fight—or wrestle.

"OK," Dempsey finally said with a shrug. "Let's get this over with."

In less than three minutes it was over. Big Ed, the kind of guy whose knuckles dragged on the ground as he walked, knotted Dempsey's legs like pieces of string. Twice Ed threw Kid Blackie to the floor. The two consecutive falls caused the referee to signal an end to the fight. Big Ed had won. Worse, neither Dempsey nor Malloy received a penny. It was, after all, a winner-take-all deal.

Kicking their bad luck, the two friends wandered around Olathe all night. "What a robbery," growled Malloy.

"And they didn't even use guns," Dempsey added.

Near dawn, the pair came to the Olathe rail yards. Two freight trains sat idling. Without a word, Malloy climbed on a northbound freight. Dempsey hopped on one going south.

As the trains moved out of the yard, the boxer and his manager waved. It would be the last time they would see each other.

CHAPTER X

Salida

"When do you want me to put this guy in your lap?"

Jack Dempsey spent part of the summer of 1916 in New York City trying to close in on his dream. Instead, he found a nightmare.

An unscrupulous manager named John "the Barber" Reisler pushed Dempsey into fights in New York where he didn't belong, for winnings that he never received. Not only did Dempsey find it difficult to make a name or money in New York, but in his final fight there, on July 14, 1916, against John Lester Johnson, Dempsey suffered three broken ribs.

Returning West to heal, Dempsey didn't fight again until November 28, 1916, in Salida, Colorado. It would be Kid Blackie's last fight in his home state.

Salida at the time was the railroad capital of the Colorado Rockies. Located in the upper Arkansas Valley, the town was a center for the Denver and Rio Grande, as well as the Atchison, Topeka & Santa Fe railroads. Salida means "gateway" in Spanish and that is what the rail town was: a major junction point. Both narrow-gauge and standard lines converged in Salida. The community boasted a teeming roundhouse and a large, railroad-operated hospital.

Salida's railroad status caused it to develop a prosperous red-light district along Front Street, later renamed Sackett Street. Front Street saw more than its share of action. A city marshal named Jim Meadows was gunned down in a saloon there.

Railroad activity in Salida began to disappear after World War II. As the railroad vanished, so did people who remembered Jack Dempsey's visit. Today, only two men living in Salida can recall much about Dempsey. But what the two do recall has significant meaning in their lives.

Harold R. Koster has been overseeing the same insurance and real estate company on Salida's First Street for more than sixty years. And Koster lived in the town even before that. He first came to Salida in 1916, shortly before Dempsey arrived.

A big, jovial man with a thick thatch of white hair, Koster was born in Yonkers, New York. He still works eight hours a day in an office lined with musty ledgers and photographs of Republican friends such as Ronald Reagan.

Koster originally came to Salida to visit a sister. "Oh, my aching back, Salida was a tough town then," he says, twiddling his necktie. "I can remember walking up from the depot. There were gambling places all over. The day I arrived I passed this Greek card joint and a man there was shot."

Harold Koster never went to college—"I got no sense or brains," he jokes—but one would never know it by his successes. He served in the Colorado House of Representatives, founded the Salida Golf Club and the town's Rotary Club, bought land and made handsome profits.

During his early days in Salida, Koster met Laura Evans, one of Colorado's most famous madams and a woman who figures in Jack Dempsey's brief relationship with the town.

From St. Louis by way of Leadville, Laura Evans set up shop in Salida at the beginning of the twentieth century. A colorful woman who rolled her own cigarettes and swore like a ranch hand, Laura Evans operated houses of prostitution around Salida's Front Street until Chaffee County authorities finally shut her down in 1950.

"Don't ask me how well I knew Laura Evans, OK?" Koster lets loose with a laugh that sounds like a train going into a tunnel. "A lot of people in this town were afraid of Laura Evans. A lot of people didn't like her. But I did. She was honest and kind. I respected her. Miss Laura had cows and she was always giving milk to poor children. During the flu epidemic of 1918 she sent her girls around town to work as nurses."

Soon after he arrived in Salida in the fall of 1916, Dempsey took a job as janitor at Laura Evans' house. It wasn't that Dempsey needed female companionship. The spring before, he had met, in Salt Lake City, Maxine Cates, a dance-hall prostitute and piano player fifteen years his senior. When Dempsey returned from New York City that summer, his confidence shaken, Maxine buoyed his spirits. Dempsey surely must have been thinking of her when he was in Salida, for the couple had been married little more than a month before his fight in that Colorado community. Yet he left Maxine in Salt Lake with his parents (who were still together, but were soon to be divorced). Dempsey's marriage to Maxine, the first of his four wives, lasted two tumultuous years.

More than likely Dempsey stayed at Laura Evans' house because he had felt comfortable around ladies of the evening ever since his days at Big Billy's in Telluride. Certainly Laura Evans was glad to have him. "She admired him," remembers Koster. "He did her handiwork at home. And he was there in case anybody caused trouble."

Through a Salida promoter named Sam Roney, Dempsey, acting now as his own manager, set up the Salida fight. His opponent was a local boxer named Hector Conrew (pronounced "Con-row"), better known as "Young Hector." Just as there were many Western fighters of that day with the name "Kid," as in Kid Blackie, so too were there fighters who called themselves "Young," as in Young Herman, Young Spence and Young Hector.

A 200-pound railroad machinist, Young Hector Conrew had faced mostly Salida fighters in his career. Nonetheless, he agreed to take on Dempsey, perhaps because Dempsey weighed only 168 pounds at the time.

The bout was held at The Rink, a combination dance hall and roller skating parlor. Once a week however, The Rink became a boxing arena that attracted high-rolling bettors from as far away as Denver. Harold Koster recalls a wealthy oilman dropping dead at The Rink during a boxing match. "Too much excitement."

Young Hector lasted three rounds against Dempsey. "A mismatch," says Koster, who sat in the audience that night close to Laura Evans.

Dempsey let Young Hector hit him a few times during the first and second rounds. In the third round, according to Harold Koster, Dempsey turned to Laura Evans and asked, "When do you want me to put this guy in your lap?"

"I don't know," said the madam with a yawn, "but I'm getting tired."

Following a clinch, Hector lost his balance and Dempsey attacked. A punch to the solar plexus, followed by more body blows, sent Hector through the ropes.

"Do you know where he lands?" asks Koster, roaring

"A mismatch," remembers Harold Koster of *Dempsey's 1916 fight in Salida.*

again with laughter. "Right in Laura Evans' lap. End of fight."

The Salida *Mountain Mail* of November 29, 1916, described the action this way:

> Young Jack Dempsey demonstrated here tonight that he is of championship calibre when he hung a knockout punch on Young Hector of this city, knocking him through the ropes for a count of 10 and 30 minutes of sleep.

The memory of that evening dampens Harold Koster's eyes. Simply, thoughts of Jack Dempsey remind Koster of Laura Evans, a woman Koster says he will never forget. When Koster first came to Salida, he tipped his hat to Miss Evans on the street, as he did to all women. Some Salidans warned Koster, a stalwart Episcopalian and a married man, that acknowledging Laura Evans in public would hurt his insurance business. Koster tipped his hat to her anyway, his entire life.

Laura Evans died at age ninety in 1953. She left a trunk containing some old photographs with a note that said the items were to be given to "the man who tipped his hat to a prostitute."

"I've still got the pictures," says Koster, leaning back in an ancient wooden armchair in his office. A framed photograph of Laura Evans hangs above his desk, right alongside one of George Bush.

And Laura Evans' house? It's now the Mon-Ark Shriner Club.

But Salida hasn't forgotten her. Each June the town, with tongue firmly planted in cheek, holds the Laura Evans Memorial Bed Race.

"Hector Conrew was clearly out of his class against Dempsey," says Earl Taliaferro, a short, bespectacled man with merry eyes and missing fingers.

"When Jack Dempsey socked you," says Taliaferro, "you stayed socked. Dempsey's best punch? Both hands."

A Salida native, Taliaferro was fifteen when Dempsey came to town. Taliaferro didn't attend the fight: he was not allowed into The Rink. "We kids didn't have much money. They figured they were gonna sell out and they did."

Taliaferro stood outside The Rink awaiting the outcome of that bout. He would have stood all night. Jack Dempsey was his hero.

Dempsey did not yet have a national reputation in the fall of 1916, but to the young people of Salida he was big news. When Earl Taliaferro and his friends heard that Dempsey would be in town for a couple of weeks, they ran over to Steve Olmstead's pool hall. Most afternoons during his stay in Salida, Dempsey got up a game of Kelly pool at Olmstead's.

"I don't remember if Dempsey was a good player," says Taliaferro, who lives on a tree-shaded street near downtown Salida. "But I do remember something unusual. Dempsey didn't place his pea number in his pants pocket as most other Kelly pool players did. He stuck it behind his ear."

Once in a while Dempsey invited people to watch him train in a room above the Salida firehouse. On one occasion Taliaferro went to the firehouse, where he witnessed a sparring session between Dempsey and Joe Fuller, an ex-miner from Cripple Creek.

"The important thing to me about Jack Dempsey," says Taliaferro, "is that he'd talk to us kids. That's what made him a hero."

Taliaferro grew up around boxing. His father, Lawrence, ran a restaurant near the Salida rail yards. Taliaferro remembers as a boy seeing Jim Flynn, the famed "Pueblo Fireman," drop into his father's restaurant. "He'd take off his fireman's clothes," says Taliaferro, "and wait on customers and wash dishes. Quite a guy." Flynn, a fireman for the railroad, was a frequent visitor to Salida. In 1904 Flynn fought twice in the town — against Harry Peppers and Ed McCory. Salida was a boxing hub during those days. Even the local dentist, Doc Wilson, duked it out with opponents on his days off.

The day after the Dempsey fight, Taliaferro rushed to Olmstead's. Sam Roney was there describing the bout to those who hadn't seen it. An engineer on the Denver and Rio Grande, Roney knew boxing. "That fellow Dempsey's got the fastest hands I ever seen," said Roney excitedly. "Great combinations. He's gonna go a long way."

Dempsey earned $250 for his night at The Rink. Coincidentally, his bout was one of the last held at the old skating hall. After Dempsey left town, Earl Taliaferro and his friends gathered for a time in school chum Warren Beck's backyard. "Warren had the only pair of boxing gloves," remembers Taliaferro, settling himself in a rocker on his big front porch. "Whoever wore Warren's gloves used to pretend he was Jack Dempsey. Quite a guy."

After helping his father in the restaurant business for two decades, Earl Taliaferro served as a county commissioner and then sold lawn mowers for a time. "I wasn't a real good boxer and I wasn't a real good lawn mower salesman, either," he says with a giggle. "See this hand? I cut off the two fingers with a lawn mower."

Quite a guy.

Salida commemorates Jack Dempsey in a way that is done nowhere else in Colorado. A half block from Harold Koster's office stands the baronial Elks Lodge 808. The lodge sponsored the Young Hector/Dempsey bout. Hanging on a hallway wall of the building, among photographs of former Elks officers, is a rectangular trophy case honoring the biggest prizefight in the town's history.

A longtime Elks member, Harold Koster never tires of walking down the street to look at that case. Examining it once more, he says, "It's something, isn't it?"

Inside the case is a pair of brown felt boxing trunks—size thirty-two—that Dempsey wore in the fight. The trunks bear a small blood stain—Young Hector's blood more than likely. Resting below the trunks is a Frisbee-sized ring gong, struck only five times during the fight.

"The rope used to be down in the club basement," explains Koster. He peers closely at the silver gong. "But now I understand it's in storage. It's still in pretty good shape, the rope. Real thick. Jack Dempsey must have been a pretty strong guy to knock somebody through it."

And into Laura Evans' lap.

CHAPTER XI

Pueblo

"If you wanna know anything about young Jack Dempsey, you gotta know about Fireman Jim Flynn."

Throughout Jack Dempsey's Colorado days, one opponent's name, Jim Flynn, reappears often. After Dempsey, Flynn was certainly Colorado's best heavyweight fighter ever. Not only that, Flynn was the only man to ever knock out Jack Dempsey.

Jim Flynn began boxing professionally in 1901. During the next twenty-five years, he fought some of the best fighters of the early part of this century: Tommy Burns, Sam Langford, Billy Papke, Philadelphia Jack O'Brien, Jack Twin Sullivan, Luther McCarthy, Carl Morris, Gunboat Smith, Jack Dillon, and Battling Levinsky.

As another in a line of Great White Hopes, Flynn fought black champion Jack Johnson twice. In 1907, Johnson stopped Flynn in the eleventh round. Five years later they fought again. This time it took Johnson nine rounds to beat Flynn in a fight that was stopped by police in Las Vegas, New Mexico.

Though born in Hoboken, New Jersey, Flynn spent most of his life in Pueblo, Colorado. Early in his career he acquired the nickname "The Pueblo Fireman," or, more often, "Fireman Jim Flynn."

Fireman Jim fought Jack Dempsey twice. Curiously, neither bout took place in Colorado. The first fight, on February 13, 1917, was held in Murray, Utah. Coincidentally, Dempsey had been training in Flynn's hometown of Pueblo when an erstwhile promoter named Fred Winsor summoned Dempsey to Utah. Dempsey had little money at the time and needed a big paycheck. Flynn, though on the downswing of his career, was still a widely recognized heavyweight, particularly in the Rocky Mountains.

But more than the money, Dempsey needed a fight. And

after the debacle of New York City, he needed to rebuild his confidence. Dempsey, sixteen years younger, figured he should be able to beat Fireman Jim Flynn, a short, pudgy man with a thick midsection and a reputation for fighting dirty.

It didn't happen. Four hundred persons watched Flynn deck Dempsey three times in the first round. Only Dempsey's youth and stamina enabled him to get back on his feet before the count of ten.

After the third knockdown, however, with a minute remaining in round one, Bernie Dempsey, who was serving as his brother's cornerman, threw a towel into the ring, signaling surrender and a TKO.

"What the heck did you do that for?" Dempsey asked his brother angrily in the dressing room afterward. "I was just getting my second wind. You chucked away my chances of ever becoming champion."

"You'd never be champion," said Bernie, "if he killed you."

That bout is the only black mark on Jack Dempsey's ring record. Though some people called the fight a fake, Dempsey steadfastly denied it. "Dough meant a lot," he said, "but it wouldn't ever make me blow a fight."

The first Jim Flynn fight made news because Dempsey had been to New York City and had tried to break into the big leagues. Though Dempsey had struck out in New York, going there had given him a reputation. Flynn's manager, a shrewd sort, decided to capitalize on this fact and spread the outcome of the bout to the media. What followed were some extremely dark days for Jack Dempsey.

A rematch with Flynn was held almost a year later to the day, on February 14, 1918, at Fort Sheridan, Illinois. Dempsey, by now seasoned with nearly twelve months' worth of bouts in the San Francisco-Oakland area, knocked out Fireman Jim Flynn in the first round. Dempsey had learned something important in the first Flynn fight: to warm up. He had gone into the ring cold and stiff. Thereafter, Dempsey embarked on a pre-fight ritual of shadowboxing for fifteen minutes in his dressing room.

Pueblo's Jim Flynn (shown with his son) gave
Dempsey some of his stiffest competition.

Though Dempsey never fought Flynn in Colorado, he knew the Fireman's old stamping ground well. He had many good friends in Pueblo. In fact, Pueblo was the first place Dempsey thought of going after departing New York City following his disastrous debut there in the summer of 1916.

On the way to Pueblo, Dempsey stopped off in Kansas City to pick up a little pocket money. Offering himself as a sparring partner for Carl Morris, a part-Irish, part-Cherokee heavyweight contender and "the Original White Hope," Dempsey was hired immediately. When the Morris training camp suddenly folded unexpectedly, Dempsey pushed on for Pueblo.

Upon arriving in Pueblo, Dempsey went quickly to Martin's Saloon, a favorite hangout, to look for a package of boxing gear—trunks, shoes and tights—that he'd left behind with Morris in Kansas City and had asked to be forwarded. The package had been sent to Pueblo—but COD. Dempsey did not have the eighty-nine cents in postage due. To raise the money, he bummed dimes and quarters around Pueblo.

The incident embarrassed Dempsey deeply. He had sparred with Morris for seventy-five cents a day; he had given his body to the man. In appreciation Morris had billed him.

"Someday I'm going to get that Carl Morris," Dempsey told his Pueblo friends. Eventually Dempsey did get Morris. Three times he fought and beat the big boxer, who outweighed him by nearly sixty pounds. On December 16, 1918, Dempsey steamrolled Morris in the first round in New Orleans. That bout finished Carl Morris' career; Dempsey's had only begun.

If Carl Morris had ever fought in Pueblo, he would have discovered a red-hot boxing town. Early in this century, sportswriter Damon Runyon, reared in Pueblo, worked for the *Chieftain* and occasionally covered fights and exhibitions in "the Steel City," as Pueblo was known. Several events bind Runyon and Dempsey. Like Dempsey, Runyon also did a tour of gold camps Victor and Cripple Creek, only not as a boxer. Runyon went there to report on mine strikes. Later, as a reporter for the Colorado Springs *Gazette,* Runyon covered a fight between Duke Nally and Jim Flynn. Still later, in 1917 in San Francisco, Runyon met Dempsey for the first time. Dempsey then was working as a janitor in a nightclub. One look at the sinewy custodian and Runyon had a nickname for him: The Manassa Mauler.

In New York, where Runyon penned the musical *Guys and Dolls*, among other works, the writer revived the nickname and became close friends with Dempsey. Runyon would often patrol the boxer's Broadway restaurant in search of stories and characters.

When Dempsey won the heavyweight title in 1919 over Jess Willard, Runyon had long since left the *Chieftain*. Pueblo's other daily newspaper, the *Star-Journal,* posted the results of that fight, round by round, on a large lighted board outside the newspaper office. When Willard failed to leave his corner in the fourth round, thousands of Puebloans stood under the *Star-Journal's* sign and cheered. Russell Battaglia was among them.

At age eighty-four, Russell Battaglia still cuts hair in his barbershop across the street from Pueblo's ornate, Victorian-style Union Station. Because he recently underwent cataract operations and hip surgery, Battaglia only gives about a half-dozen haircuts a day. But he works every day.

"I can't stay home and rot," says Battaglia, a small man with thinning brown hair. His current barbershop, which he's owned since 1950, is as spotless as its owner's high-gloss white loafers.

Born in Sicily in 1900, Russell Battaglia came to Pueblo with his father, Joseph, from New Orleans in 1903. Like many Europeans, Joseph Battaglia had been drawn to Pueblo because of its prosperous steel mills. The senior Battaglia built a barbershop in his home. When his son was ten, Joseph Battaglia built something else: a raised platform so little Russ could learn to cut hair.

As a seventh grader in 1913, Russell Battaglia heard for the first time the name Jack Dempsey. Beginning in late 1912, Dempsey had been coming to Pueblo now and then to train and to look for fights.

"Kid Blackie will be champion of the world some day," announced Buck Weaver, then a Pueblo barber with an avid interest in boxing.

Playing hookey from Pueblo's Central School, Battaglia would sneak over to Shorty Adams' Second Class Saloon on South Union Avenue. The tavern is now Johnson Electric Company. Because Shorty Adams did not allow children into his establishment, Battaglia would sit at the rear of the building, atop a big ice box, and watch Dempsey train. "Hello, son," Dempsey would call out.

"Those words," remembers Battaglia, "would keep my heart thumping for a week."

If Battaglia admired Dempsey, he idolized Jim Flynn. "If you wanna know anything about young Jack Dempsey," says Battaglia, taking an empty seat in his barbershop, "you gotta know about Fireman Jim Flynn."

Flynn was an Italian, and that, admits Battaglia, was one reason why the barber liked him so much. "His real name was Andrew Chiariglione. His father, Hector, was founder and publisher of the Italian weekly newspaper in Pueblo. Flynn and my father were the same age; both were born in 1879."

When Russell Battaglia bought his first barbershop in Pueblo, the shop stood at 317 West Northern. A tailor shop now occupies the site. Battaglia purchased that shop from Buck Weaver, once Dempsey's manager. In the yard behind the shop, Weaver had set up a boxing ring. All sorts of fighters used to come to that backyard ring to work out. And because the shop was located in Bessemer, a rough-and-tough smelter, brickyard and packinghouse neighborhood, all the fighters who dropped in were hard-nosed: men like Eddie Johnson, Sam Greer, Kid Max, Mike Pason, Joe "the Wop" Kelly and Mexican Pete Everett. Perhaps the most hard-nosed of all was Jim Flynn.

"Flynn was a slugger," says Battaglia, getting up slowly from his chair to wait on a customer. "Dempsey was a hard hitter, but Flynn always went for all the marbles when he swung. He tried to knock your block off."

Though Battaglia remembers with fondness Dempsey working out, the Pueblo barber never actually saw Dempsey fight. However, he did see Jim Flynn in the ring. In 1921, Battaglia witnessed a charity bout at Pueblo's Mineral Park: Jim Flynn versus Mexican Pete Everett. The fight benefited Pueblo, which that year suffered tremendous damage from a flood.

"Both guys," says Battaglia of the 1921 fight, "were old and fat by then."

An earlier fight pitted Flynn against Tony Ross at the Pueblo Opera House. That contest was held on the Fourth of July, a holiday favored by many prizefight promoters in the early part of this century.

"Flynn got that decision," says Battaglia. "But Ross thought it was rigged. He challenged Flynn to fight again the next day. Bareknuckles. They went at it over at Minnequa Park, a big amusement place. I can't recall who won."

Battaglia saw Fireman Jim fight—and drink. "One time Flynn socked a guy named Clarence Hagen clear across my barbershop. I don't know if Flynn had a drinking problem, but when he had a drink he was tough. I didn't want to be around him then. He was a regular street brawler."

Flynn was also something of a ladies' man, according to Battaglia. Fireman Jim preferred Pueblo's Vail Hotel. Perhaps because his brother was a Hollywood movie director, Flynn frequently checked into the Vail (a fancy hostelry remodeled in the summer of 1984) with a film actress in tow.

Flynn, who was five feet, eight inches tall and weighed 185 pounds, had sandy hair and a light complexion. Battaglia figures Flynn must have been part Irish; he even called himself "Andrew Haymes" for a while. "He sure didn't look Italian. In those days lots of fighters were taking Irish names. It was the thing to do, like fighting on the Fourth of July."

Dempsey, on the other hand, with inky hair and a smoky complexion, *looked* Italian.

To confound matters, Jim Flynn's manager at one point was a character named "Abdulla the Turk."

Flynn fell on hard times after he quit boxing. "He drove a cab in Phoenix for a while," Battaglia reports. "Then he started to go blind. He died broke; spent all his money." Flynn died on April 12, 1935, at the age of fifty-five.

Setting down his clippers, Battaglia offers a footnote. "Those last years when Fireman Jim was suffering, when he needed cash, do you know who helped him? Jack Dempsey, that's who."

After *he* retired from the ring, Dempsey on occasion returned to Pueblo. And when he did he would often go to Battaglia's shop and request "the works"—haircut, shave, massage, shampoo—for $3.50. "His beard was like wire," says Battaglia. "I had to work to cut it." Today, haircuts at Russell Battaglia's run five dollars. "The works" has been discontinued.

The last time Battaglia saw Dempsey was in 1959. Battaglia had gone to Chicago for a barber's convention. "Someone in our hotel told me that Jack Dempsey was in the lobby. 'I know him,' I said, so I went down. I pushed my way to the front, there was this big crowd, see, and I said, 'I'm Russ Battaglia, from Pueblo, and I worked for Buck Weaver.' He said, 'Great, great,' and then I was pushed away. The line around him was about five deep. I'm a little guy so I didn't have much of a chance.''

Battaglia says he wanted to be a boxer as a kid but long hours at the barber chair left him little time to train. His size—five feet, three inches—didn't help him, either. "I'm even shorter now.''

These days, Battaglia's boxing interests are confined mostly to Dempsey and Jim Flynn. "Jack Dempsey was in my opinion the greatest fighter who ever lived. Flynn was the wildest." Flynn once gave Battaglia a pair of boxing gloves, a medicine ball and a punching bag. "A barber who worked for me took them. I wish I had them. But I do have Flynn," says Battaglia, pointing to his head, "up here. I've

As a kid, Pueblo's Russell Battaglia cut school to watch Dempsey work out. Years later he cut the boxer's hair.

never forgotten him. Whenever I think of Jack Dempsey, I think of old Fireman Jim.''

Living on the eleventh floor of a fashionable senior citizens' high-rise apartment building in Pueblo is a tall, dapper man with an imperial face. Born the year Benjamin Harrison was president, Clyde O'Neal is still fit, vigorous and debonair looking.

With a shock of snowy-white hair and a gravelly voice, O'Neal resembles another O'Neill—Tip.

Although Pueblo has a population under 100,000, Clyde O'Neal does not know Russell Battaglia. The two have always run in different circles. While Battaglia spent most of his life around Pueblo's steel mill crowd, O'Neal grew up in farming country east of town. Later, he made his fortune in downtown real estate investments. Clyde O'Neal is old money.

O'Neal and his family came to Colorado in 1895 from Arkansas. His father suffered from a bronchial condition. At first the O'Neals lived in Guffey, Colorado, until the mines there closed. Then they moved to Avondale and finally to Vineland, ten miles east of Pueblo, where they farmed beets and hay. "It was a very hard life in Vineland," says O'Neal, "But my father was determined to make it."

Young Clyde farmed on his own in La Junta and Hobson, Colorado. When his father died in 1916, he returned to Vineland to run the family spread. O'Neal had met Jack Dempsey in 1914. The O'Neal farm was about a mile from property owned by two eccentric brothers, Orly and Jack Fisher. Orly, nicknamed "Liz" for reasons unknown, was Dempsey's old hoboing companion. During late 1913, the Fishers befriended Dempsey. It was on their farm that O'Neal first saw the boxer.

"Dempsey was a likable fellow, and strong. I watched him butcher a hog and then throw the animal over his shoulder like it was a piece of dry cleaning."

Though their background was agriculture, the Fisher brothers had dreams of making it as sports promoters. In fact, they believed in Jack Dempsey when few others did.

Like Buck Weaver and countless more Coloradans had done, the Fishers became Dempsey's managers.

In the mornings, O'Neal caught glimpses of Dempsey doing roadwork. "He'd get out there by himself, while Jack and Liz slept, and run around a square in Vineland. It's about four and one-half miles altogether. Dempsey wasn't a drinker or smoker. He couldn't have been. Not to run that distance."

When Dempsey wasn't pounding the pavement in Vineland, he was looking for fights in Pueblo. "He'd fight anybody for five dollars, or at least that's what he said," recalls O'Neal. "I used to go to all the fights. There wasn't anything else to do in Colorado in those days."

The problem was that no one wanted to fight Dempsey, especially not for five dollars. The Fishers couldn't sign their fighter to a bout. They made most of their attempts at Dixon Miller's, a Pueblo pool hall and cigar store. Owned by Fred Dixon and Ed Miller, the hall, like Shorty Adams' saloon, also held a boxing ring.

"Dixon and Miller," says O'Neal, "didn't think Dempsey—he was Kid Blackie back then, if I'm not mistaken—was worth much. Jack had a desire. He loved to fight. But nobody really was interested in a kid of twenty."

On July 4, 1919, O'Neal encountered Liz Fisher on the outskirts of Pueblo. The two hadn't seen each other in some time. O'Neal asked Fisher to join him for a ride to Rye, Colorado, thirty-five miles southwest.

While in Rye, the pair heard the news: Dempsey had beaten Jess Willard to win the world heavyweight title.

"Liz," O'Neal said, turning to his friend. "Four years ago you were Dempsey's manager. Don't you wish you had him now?"

"Let's go home," answered Fisher. "I feel sick."

As a longtime regional manager for Mutual of New York Life Insurance Company, Clyde O'Neal frequently traveled to the East Coast. On those trips he would often stop at Jack Dempsey's restaurant in Manhattan. "He'd always ask me about Liz Fisher and Dixon Miller's," says O'Neal, staring out his apartment window. "Dempsey had a hard time of it while he was in Pueblo, but I don't think he was ever bitter about it. Those days probably toughened him, if anything."

Dixon Miller's is now a vacant building. The Fisher brothers are gone, too. Jack Fisher ran a bar near Las Vegas, Nevada, and did become a sports promoter of sorts:

he wrote the rules for dog-racing tracks. Liz Fisher died in Pueblo after retiring from the Missouri Pacific Railroad. He'd been a conductor.

"The Fishers made a little money, I'd guess," says O'Neal, who knows something about finances. "But if they'd kept Dempsey on a leash, they would have made a whole lot more."

CHAPTER XII

Denver

"There'll never be another like him."

Following a brief exhibition in 1920 at the Denver Stockyards, in which he quickly leveled two opponents, Jack Dempsey put Colorado boxing and Kid Blackie behind him.

Dempsey did, however, return to Colorado on occasion, mostly to fish the Gunnison and Conejos rivers. He spent a few weeks in August, 1921, resting at Antonito Rainbow Trout Lodges, near his birthplace in Manassa. "The conqueror of Carpentier has thus far refused to discuss pugilism publicly," reported the *Rocky Mountain News* of that visit. "What he says to his relatives and old-time friends they keep to themselves."

Prior to his first fight with Gene Tunney, in July of 1926, Dempsey trained for a week at The Broadmoor in Colorado Springs, courtesy of the inn's owner, Spencer Penrose. During Dempsey's stay at the resort, the press dogged him relentlessly, thanks to media-minded Spec Penrose. After attempting to run up Cheyenne Mountain, but only lasting a few hundred yards, Dempsey decided The Broadmoor wasn't for him.

In 1940, when he stopped giving boxing exhibitions, Dempsey began a career refereeing wrestling matches. He came to Salida in 1941 to officiate a match at the high school. He did the same in Pueblo three years later.

Denver figured in many of Dempsey's return trips to Colorado. Dempsey had always liked Denver ever since his teenage years. During the Kid Blackie days, when he briefly knocked around Larimer Street, Dempsey managed to meet several of Denver's notables, including famed writer Gene Fowler, author of *Timber Line*. Prior to winning the heavyweight championship in 1919, Dempsey met Harry Tammen and Fred Bonfils, colorful owners of the *Denver Post*.

Tammen and Bonfils were two of the first people to feel that Dempsey had a chance to beat Jess Willard. Another who believed Dempsey had a good shot against Willard was the *Post's* sports editor, Otto Floto.

A bullet-headed, wooden-legged raconteur, Otto Floto was an authority on boxing. For a short time he managed Bob Fitzsimmons, once the world's heavyweight titleholder. Coincidentally, Floto acted as a boxing promoter in Cripple Creek, during the 1890s. He would scour the saloons along Cripple's Bennett Avenue for fighting drunks, then prop the men up on the stage of the Butte Opera House and charge a dollar for admission.

Floto also happened to be a close friend of Gene Fowler as well as the onetime boss of Damon Runyon. For years Floto liked people to believe that he owned the Sills-Floto Circus, which was in actuality owned by the *Denver Post*. The newspaper used Floto's name because it had a nice ring to it.

More than anything, Otto Floto was a writer of purple prose. When Bill Naughton, a well-known boxing commentator, died in California, Floto wrote, "As we stand upon the threshold of grief this melancholy morn, there is an increased secretion of our lachrymal glands."

Floto and Jack Dempsey are forever bound in history by an event that occurred in 1915. For a short period that year Floto managed Kid Blackie. Floto arranged a series of bouts, one right after the other, in Gunnison. All the bouts took place on payday, when money was plentiful.

It was an exhausting experience for Dempsey, but profitable enough for him and Floto to earn six hundred dollars. On their way out of Gunnison, the pair decided to take a roundabout way back to Denver. More action might exist in Grand Junction, Floto decided.

The action came before they wanted it. On a lonely mountain road, four gunmen on horseback stopped Floto's touring car. The bandits ordered Dempsey and Floto out of the vehicle. After threatening to shoot the two travelers, the gunmen took their money.

The incident represented for Dempsey one more time someone had robbed him of his boxing winnings. Disconsolate, he and Floto made their way to Grand Junction. They still had a few dollars stuffed in their shoes, so they went to the Grand Junction Hotel and Lunch Room for a bite. Sitting down at the table, Dempsey noticed that the customers across the dining room seemed familiar.

"Aren't those the guys that robbed us?" Dempsey asked.

"I don't know," said Floto, unwilling to get involved.

But Dempsey didn't need another opinion. He went straight for the bandits. Taking them by surprise, Dempsey punched all four before they knew what hit them. A "destructive dervish," Floto later wrote. Dempsey grabbed the gun and tossed it across the restaurant floor. Then he found his money. Otto Floto didn't move.

Eddie Bohn, perhaps Jack Dempsey's best friend in the world, has lived in Denver for more than eighty years. Bohn sparred with Dempsey, drank with him, and gave him shelter. Now Bohn owns a shrine to the boxer.

The Pig 'n Whistle Motel and Restaurant, an aging piece of art deco, sits on West Colfax Avenue a few miles from the Denver Broncos' football stadium. The faded flamingo-pink motor court has seen better days. The horseshoe-shaped swimming pool is cracked and empty most of the time now. The motel's California style tile roof is crumbling. But there is still great pride in the place, mostly because Jack Dempsey slept there.

Tall, jug-eared, and gruff as a wakened bear, Eddie Bohn was born in Denver in 1902. With money he made as a professional prizefighter, Bohn opened the Pig 'n Whistle in 1924—"the same day as Jack's birthday, June 24." For years the motel and restaurant served as a gathering spot for celebrities traveling through Denver. A Colorado state senator from 1936-1940, and a sports guru all his life, Bohn catered to personalities, expecially athletes.

"Jack was here about twenty times or more, I'd guess," says Bohn, walking toward the rear of the single-story, forty-unit motel. "Lots of times I never told anybody, the press or nobody, that Jack was here. He wanted peace and quiet. He'd stay a week. He liked our pool. He'd sit around it and go swimming at midnight."

Room No. 39, at the back of the motel, is indeed peaceful and quiet. Bohn stops, pulls out a key and opens a sliding glass door. "This is our Jack Dempsey Room," he says, pushing aside a curtain and entering the room.

The interior of No. 39 resembles a normal-looking motel room: two double beds, white and blue bedspreads, TV, yellow vinyl chairs and table, regular bath. On one cinder block wall hangs a generic landscape. On another wall, a poster indicates that the room is the Jack Dempsey Room. The poster says that many boxers stayed there, including Max Baer, Primo Carnera, Tony Galento, Barney Ross, Gene Fullmer, Carmen Basilio and Jim Braddock. In fact, all sorts of luminaries checked into Room 39: Clint Eastwood, Roy Rogers, Tommy Dorsey.

Locking the room Bohn doubles back across the motel walkway and ducks into the restaurant next door. Though the restaurant is built around the Three Little Pigs theme—a mural on one wall details the nursery rhyme—the bar adjoining the restaurant is ultra-masculine: a swordfish and boxing gloves adorn one wall.

In the hall connecting the restaurant's dining room and bar is a photograph gallery containing pictures of Jack Dempsey and anyone else Eddie Bohn felt like including. A snapshot display documents the Jack Dempsey Day in Manassa in 1966, an event Bohn helped to organize. Nearby, a photo shows Bohn inducting Dempsey into the Colorado Sports Hall of Fame in 1965. Another photo reveals Dempsey at his New York restaurant with Bohn, and one next to that has Dempsey at Bohn's Colorado restaurant. A framed newspaper advertisement, circa 1920, announces a fight between George Coplen of Cripple Creek and Johnny Capelli of Dillon, Colorado. The fight is to be held at the American Legion Hall in Canon City, Colorado. "Both of these men," the ad states, "have met noted pugilists, including Jack Dempsey."

There is a photograph of Dempsey, with Bohn's two young sons, in his Coast Guard uniform in 1945, and one of Dempsey with a pony he gave the Bohn boys. A framed note from Deanna Dempsey, Jack's fourth wife, sent to Bohn after her husband's death in 1983, says: "He loved you, Eddie, like a brother or better. Your flowers with 'Pal' would have touched his heart."

Eddie Bohn didn't attend Dempsey's funeral. "I couldn't," he says. "I didn't feel too well. Besides, they wanted it private."

Still, Deanna Dempsey called Bohn the night her husband died in their New York apartment at the age of eighty-seven. In fact, Bohn was the first person Mrs. Dempsey notified.

Denver's Eddie Bohn: "Jack never learned to block punches. He just punched. That was how he blocked."

Eddie Bohn met Dempsey in 1923 at the San Pedro Gymnasium in Los Angeles. Dempsey was looking for sparring partners, men who would train with him in exhibitions up and down the West Coast. The pay was one hundred dollars a round, a huge sum for that time.

"I told Jack I was from Colorado," says Bohn, sliding into a red booth in the bar of his Pig 'n Whistle. Above the booth is an oil painting of Dempsey. "Colorado was the magic word. We got along right after that."

Bohn estimates he sparred at least one hundred rounds with Dempsey. "He wore big, twenty-ounce gloves so he wouldn't hurt his sparring partners. The other guy wore fourteen-ounce gloves. If Jack didn't wear the big gloves he'd knock a guy's brains out." Indeed, sparring partners were said to be taking a risk with Dempsey. He wanted the ring to himself, even in practice.

Dempsey would, says Bohn, hit a sparring partner as hard as he could, but never in vital spots. "He always told you he was going to hit you at least once. And then he did hit you, just to show you who was in charge."

According to Bohn, Dempsey's style was to throw a short left hook as he pivoted. "You couldn't block it. I learned the punch, but nothing like he could throw it. Jack never learned to block punches. He just punched. That was how he blocked. And you know something? He never broke his hands."

Inspecting his own hands, Bohn shakes his head. "I broke these lotsa times."

Getting up, Bohn ambles to the bar to fix himself a glass of orange juice. When he returns, he says, "Jack's mother once told me a story about how he was out in front of the house in Manassa and a kid was slugging the hell out of him and Jack wouldn't fight back. She said, 'If you don't fight I'm going to give you a licking.' She encouraged him to box. He'd been called 'Willy the Sissy.' Boxing pulled him out. He was always shy."

Years after he had retired from the ring, Dempsey took Bohn to places such as Aspen and Leadville, where he had boxed in saloons that had little fifteen-foot rings. "Jack probably had 450 fights in places like that," says Bohn. "And there's no way you could look up those fights."

The two men went together to Bailey, Colorado, where Dempsey shot a deer, and to a nursing home in La Junta to see Les Jacobs, who had been a ticket-taker in a carnival where Dempsey once worked. Bohn and Dempsey went to Pueblo during World War II to sell war bonds. Dempsey discovered that George Coplen was working at the Pueblo Army Depot. The two old fighters had a tearful reunion.

Dempsey took his friend to Cripple Creek, also. "We were there for three or four hours, just looking around," remembers Bohn. "Jack tried to find some of the places he fought. 'I was so goddamned poor here,' he told me, 'I don't even like to think about it.'

"Funny, but nobody spotted Jack in Cripple Creek. And he was so well-known. Finally we stopped for lunch. Jack ordered a bowl of soup and roast pork. The waitress said, ' You're Jack Dempsey, aren't you?' Jack said, 'Who's Dempsey?' Well, she went outside and yelled, 'Jack Dempsey's here!' In about five minutes there were seventy-five people in the restaurant wanting Jack's autograph."

Years later, as a favor to Dempsey, Bohn would sign the boxer's autograph in his absence. Taking a napkin from a nearby holder and a pen from his pocket, Bohn produces a reasonable facsimile. "I can write like him, but I could never fight like him."

Eddie Bohn's height—six feet, four and one-half inches—makes him appear too tall for a boxer. The scar tissue above his eyes and over the bridge of his nose, however, says otherwise. Bohn learned to box at the West Side Neighborhood House in Denver. He went there as a youth and saw Charlie Miller, a Golden Gloves fighter, working out.

"I told somebody I could lick that guy," says Bohn. "'You wanna try?' somebody asks me. 'Sure,' I says. I was wearing tennis shoes, which are the worst thing in the world to wear because they stick to the floor. But I didn't care. Then I got in the ring and Charlie Miller killed me. Punched me full of holes.

"A few days later I went back and Charlie showed me some things. So did Eddie Eagan, who was there and who later went to the Olympics."

Bohn fought in Elks Club bouts and Denver smokers and became the Rocky Mountain regional champion of seven states. He had sixty-two fights altogether. Ten were draws, he lost two decisions, and won the rest. No one ever knocked him out.

Bohn rises to fetch another orange juice. At the bar he tells his cook to fix him something to eat. "Jack would never take more than three drinks," Bohn says, settling back in

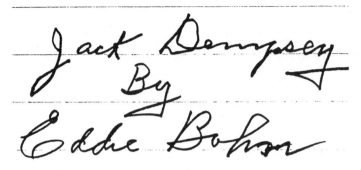

Jack Dempsey
By
Eddie Bohn

When the champ wasn't around, a Denver friend offered a hand.

the booth. "He said he was one-third Cherokee, one-third German, and one-third Scots-Irish. People with that blood mix, Jack said, got mean after three drinks."

Bohn never saw Dempsey angry. "He was a gentle man, nice in the best sense of the word." And he was a big eater who never met a meal he didn't like. His large appetite apparently stemmed from the days he spent in the kitchen of the Rio Grande Eating House. A heavyweight only has to have four moves, says Eddie Bohn: walk to the table, sit down, pull out a chair and go with both hands.

If anyone could explain why Dempsey succeeded as a boxer, it is Eddie Bohn. "He had a lot of self-discipline. He had character and principle. He weighed only 180 pounds but he was the strongest guy I ever knew. And he was a natural puncher. Ever a guy is born to be a fighter, it was him."

The 1983 made-for-television movie about Dempsey, starring Treat Williams in the title role, distressed Bohn. "First of all, it never said a thing about Dempsey's Colorado days. It never identified any of the places in the state.

"What bothered me most about that movie was that it showed Jack always a sad guy. Sure, Jack had it rough once; everybody did. But Jack was a happy man. He was fun to be with. People brought him out. He loved to joke. He'd tie

154

your shoelaces together while you were napping. And then he'd give you all the money he had when you woke up.

"Jack Dempsey had the biggest heart of anybody. There'll never be another like him."

AFTERWORD

Less than three years after leaving Colorado for the final time, Jack Dempsey became heavyweight boxing champion of the world. How did he manage the feat so quickly? Part of the answer lies with a shrewd advisor named Jack Kearns, one of eleven managers Dempsey had in his checkered career.

Realizing the boxing limitations in the Rocky Mountains, in early 1917 Dempsey traveled to northern California, where he signed on with Kearns. For the rest of that year, Dempsey fought in the Bay Area whenever Kearns could arrange it. In time, Dempsey built a solid reputation as a promising newcomer. The following year, 1918, Kearns gained Dempsey one important heavyweight bout after another, in cities from one end of the country to the other. By 1919, Dempsey was ready for a title shot against Jess Willard, which Kearns obtained.

Did Dempsey then owe everything to Jack Kearns? No. Dempsey's rapid rise to national recognition can also be traced to his enormous will to win, to his dream. During those first couple of years with Kearns, Dempsey averaged two fights a month. Often, it was Dempsey's unyielding, never-say-quit approach that kept him going at this pace. It was the same gutsiness that had saved him in Cripple Creek in 1913 against George Coplen, the same toughness that followed him until his career ended in 1927. (In terms of sheer fortitude, few moments in fistic history can match Dempsey's spectacular 1923 title fight against Luis Firpo, "The Wild Bull of the Pampas." After Firpo had smacked Dempsey through ropes and sent him flying atop reporters' typewriters, Dempsey picked himself up, climbed back in the ring and knocked out Firpo.)

Recently, two dissimilar students of pugilism analyzed the fascination Dempsey caused. Mike Tyson, current holder of a pair of heavyweight crowns, said of Dempsey on ABC-TV's *Wide World of Sports:* "He threw punches with bad intention. Dempsey was a whirlwind, an action-packed fighter with a ferociousness in him. He was a tiger and the people were not used to that type of fighting and fell in love with him."

Novelist Joyce Carol Oates, in her graceful study *On Boxing,* wonders, "Has there ever been a fighter quite like the young Dempsey?—the embodiment, it seems, of hunger, rage, the will to do hurt; the spirit of the American frontier come East to win his fortune?"

Oates goes on to theorize that it was Dempsey's ring style —swift, pitiless, always direct and percussive, that changed American boxing forever.

And put Manassa on the map.

To Jack Dempsey — the All-American Champion
with Sincere Friendship and Good Wishes
Hubert H Humphrey

Images such as Dempsey with Jimmy Durante and Hubert Humphrey, c. 1968, adorn the Dempsey Museum in Manassa.

ACKNOWLEDGMENTS

This book has its origins in an article that appeared in the *Albuquerque Journal's* weekly magazine, *Impact.* I am indebted to the *Journal's* editor, Gerald Crawford and *Impact's* editor, Pat Reed, for their initial support.

In addition to the many interviews that make up *Kid Blackie*, various people across Colorado provided information of one sort or another. They include Elizabeth Burns, *Colorado Springs Gazette Telegraph*; Bette Carnes, *Pueblo Chieftain*; Caleb Casebier, Olathe; Jim Coppfer, *Rocky Mountain News*; R.J. Davis, Olathe; Richard E. Day, *Montrose Daily Press*; Alvin Edlund, Jr., Salida Public Library; Leland Feitz, Colorado Springs; Dave Fishell, Grand Junction *Daily Sentinel*; Dona Freeman, Montrose; Eleanor Gehres, Western History Department, Denver Public Library; Marvin Gregory, Ouray; Terry Hanna, *Conejos County Citizen;* Judy Hartman, *Durango Herald;* Raymonde M. Jones, Western Research Librarian, Pueblo Library District; Muriel Marshall, Delta; Ree Mobley, Pikes Peak Library District, Colorado Springs; Arlene Shovald, Salida *Mountain Mail*; Robert and Elwood Smith, Grand Junction; Margo B. West, Colorado Historical Society, Denver; and Judy Zimmerman, Silverton Public Library.

I would also like to thank the staffs of the Albuquerque Public Library; the Center of Southwest Studies, Fort Lewis College, Durango; the La Plata County Historical Society, Durango; the Montrose County Historical Society; and the Zimmerman Library, University of New Mexico, Albuquerque.

Others deserving special gratitude are Jack Swanson of Wayfinder Press, who helped shepherd the project with cogent criticism and unflagging encouragement; Janet L.

Oslund of the Ouray Public Library, who edited the manuscript with great diligence and uncommon foresight; Rod Barker of Tesuque, New Mexico, who supplied one valuable Dempsey item and called my attention to another; Bob Wheeler of ABC-TV in New York City, who handily retrieved a piece of footage; Richard Pipes of Albuquerque, a gifted photographer who also proved an enjoyable travel and research companion; and my wife, Susan, who has gone the distance.

T.S.

SELECTED BIBLIOGRAPHY

Athearn, Robert G. *Rebel of the Rockies: A History of the Denver and Rio Grande Western Railroad.* New Haven: Yale University Press, 1962.

Bennett, Edwin Lewis. *Boom Town Boy.* Chicago: Sage Books, 1968.

Dempsey, Jack, as told to Bob Considine. *Dempsey.* New York: Simon & Schuster, 1959.

Dempsey, Jack, with Barbara Piatelli Dempsey. *Dempsey.* New York: Harper & Row, 1977.

Fleischer, Nat. *Jack Dempsey.* New Rochelle, New York: Arlington House, 1972.

_____. *The Ring Record Book and Boxing Encyclopedia.* New York: The Ring Book Shop, Inc., 1968.

Fowler, Gene. *Timber Line.* New York: Covici, Friede, 1933.

Heller, Peter, *In This Corner . . . !* New York: Simon & Schuster, 1973.

Lee, Mabel Barbee. *Back in Cripple Creek.* Garden City, New York: Doubleday & Co., 1968.

Oates, Joyce Carol. *On Boxing.* Garden City, New York: Dolphin/Doubleday, 1987.

Roberts, Randy. *Jack Dempsey: The Manassa Mauler.* Baton Rouge: Louisiana State University Press, 1979.

Rockwell, Wilson. *Uncompahgre Country.* Denver: Sage Books, 1965.

Sirica, John J. "Unforgettable Jack Dempsey." *Reader's Digest,* March, 1986, pp. 108-113.

Smith, Duane. *Rocky Mountain Boom Town: A History of Durango.* Albuquerque: University of New Mexico Press, 1980.

Smith, Toby. "The House That Jack Left." *Sport* Magazine, February, 1985. p. 13.

_____. "When Dempsey Came to Town." *Albuquerque Journal Impact Magazine,* September 18, 1984, pp. 4-9.

Sprague, Marshall. *Colorado: A Bicentennial History.* New York: Norton, 1976.

Stearns, Myron, and Jack Dempsey. *Round by Round.* New York: Whittlesey House, 1940.